CONTENTS

T0362757

More ENGLISH BASICS

NOUNS AND PRONOUNS

Nouns

A noun is a naming word.

A noun is a naming word but, as you know by now, there are different kinds of noun.

> A **common noun** is the name of people, places, creatures, objects.
>
> For example: teacher, school, toothpaste, mice.
>
> A **proper noun** is the name of a particular person, place, thing, business or organisation.
>
> For example: Kate, Rotorua, Milford Sound, The Warehouse.
>
> A **collective noun** is the name given to a group of things.
>
> For example: a <u>flock</u> of birds, a <u>fleet</u> of ships.
>
> An **abstract noun** is something you can't see, hear, touch or taste. These can be qualities, emotions or ideas.
>
> For example: courage, mana, creativity, independence.

All proper nouns start with a capital letter.

1 **Each of the following sentences has a noun in bold. In the space provided, identify the type of noun.**

a.   We were over-taken by a **gang** of noisy tourists.   _____

b.   The spilt **milk** went everywhere.   _____

c.   We had a brilliant holiday at **Martins Bay**.   _____

d.   The **trees** outside rustle in the wind.   _____

e.   It is so annoying when people text while at the dinner **table**.   _____

f.   Sarah has great **taste** in clothes.   _____

g.   **Mrs Thomas** directed her gaze at the back row.   _____

h.   It was the job of the **jury** to decide if he was guilty.   _____

Pronouns

Pronouns stand in place of nouns when referring to persons or things.

They have the same function as nouns and writers use them to save repeating the name of a person or thing too often in a sentence, passage or story.

I	we	you	us
he/she/it	him/her/it	they	them

ISBN: 9780170462990

1 **Read the following passage and circle all the** pronouns **you spot.**

Rīpeka and Riley strolled down the dirt track to the bottom of the farm. They were planning on having a dip in the river. Rīpeka liked to use the tyre swing. She would swing out and land with an almighty splash in the river.

'You are such a chicken, Riley. You would love it if you just gave it a go.'

'No way! Last week Lucas tried it, missed the jump and he ended up hitting the tree.'

'I saw him do that! It was hilarious! Why don't we give it a go today while no one is around and I will show you how to do it?' Rīpeka said.

'OK, I will do it once. You had better promise me that nothing will happen or you are in for it,' Riley said.

'I promise I will look after us. You have absolutely nothing to fear.'

Possessive pronouns
Possessive pronouns are words that signify ownership.

'Possess' means to own or to have; 'pronoun', as you know, is a word that stands in place of a noun. Instead of repeating the name of who owns something too often in a sentence, passage or story, a possessive pronoun is used.

For example, instead of: This is the cat **that belongs to me**.

   use: This cat is **my** cat.

   or: This cat is **mine**.

   instead of: This is Brianna's dinner, my dinner, Dad's dinner, Mackenna's dinner.

   use: This is **our** dinner.

Below is a list of the most commonly used possessive pronouns.

my	your	his	her	their	our	its
mine	yours		hers	theirs	ours	

1 **Underline the** possessive pronouns **in the following sentences.**

a. They let off their fireworks to celebrate the start of Matariki.

b. My mother drives a white car. She loves her car.

c. I'll let you taste my sandwich if you let me have some of yours.

d. The dog chewed its bone and then went into its kennel.

e. I told her the book was mine but she said it was the school's.

2 **Use** pronouns **and** possessive pronouns **to complete the following passage:**

_____ always believed that _____ would be a singer. My auntie told _____ that _____ must persevere and practise every day. She was a famous singer and always told _____ family all about the things she did and _____ believed her.

ISBN: 9780170462990

ADJECTIVES

Adjectives are describing words.

Adjectives are words we use to describe nouns. They add colour to what we are writing about. You don't get hungry when someone says: 'I ate steak.' But, when someone says: 'I ate a huge, succulent and juicy steak', your mouth begins to water and you maybe even feel envious.

1 **Underline the adjectives in the following sentences.**

    a.   Her bedroom wall was an awesome shade of orange.

    b.   The insect scuttled along the blank wall.

    c.   The muffins were warm, soft and full of chocolate chips – yum!

    d.   Isabel had a sleek cell phone.

    e.   Justin threw himself into a crunching tackle.

2 **Match each boring adjective with a more interesting adjective.**

tired	astounding	starving	pretty
small	fantastic	hideous	old
good	filthy	gorgeous	angry
surprising	boiling	enormous	hungry
hot	exhausted	ancient	funny
dirty	spotless	furious	ugly
clean	minuscule	hysterical	big

3 **Write a series of sentences that incorporate the following adjectives. Be creative!**

Think winter…	slippery	foggy	red	saturated
	roaring	deep	icy	raced

_____

_____

_____

Think movies…	buttery	long	dark	excellent
	comfy	chewy	hot	lazy

_____

_____

_____

ISBN: 9780170462990

COMPARATIVES

A comparative is a type of adjective that *compares* one thing with another, for example: Peter's pumpkin is bigger than Paul's.

We know that adjectives describe the noun. The comparative adjective specifically compares two things, hence the name **compar**ative. It comes from the Latin **comparere** — to match, to couple together.

There are two main rules for forming comparative adjectives:

For most short words add **er**:
For example: *hard — harder*   *soft — softer*

For most long adjectives (usually of more than one syllable) put the word **more** in front:
For example: *popular — more popular*   *beautiful — more beautiful*

1 **Underline the comparative in the following sentences.**

   a. Tony was smaller than Phillip.

   b. My t-shirt is bluer than my sister's.

   c. Doing my homework is more important than reading a magazine.

   d. I am more relaxed when swinging in my hammock than when I sit in my chair.

   e. My English teacher is crazier than my History teacher but she is more helpful with my projects.

2 **Rewrite the following adjectives in the comparative form by adding 'er' or putting the word 'more' in front.**

   a. pale

   b. nice

   c. slow

   d. clean

   e. uncomfortable

   f. interesting

   g. strict

   h. difficult

   i. complicated

   j. smooth

   k. fast

   l. easy

ISBN: 9780170462990

SUPERLATIVES

A superlative is a type of adjective that compares one thing to *all the others*, for example: Peter's pumpkin is the biggest.

We now know that the comparative adjective compares two things. The superlative, on the other hand, compares one thing with everything else. The word **super** comes from Latin and means **above** or **superior**. By using a superlative we are saying that nothing else can equal the quality of the object; it is superior to all the others whether it be good or bad.

There are two main rules for forming superlative adjectives:

For most short words add **est**:
For example: *hard — hardest*   *soft — softest*

For most long adjectives (usually of more than one syllable) put the word **most** in front:
For example: *popular — most popular*   *beautiful — most beautiful*

1   **Underline the superlative in the following sentences.**

a. This orange is the juiciest orange I have eaten.

b. That was the stupidest thing he had ever done.

c. Charlie Tangaroa is my most favourite fictional character.

d. That was the worst movie I've seen.

e. She said I was the most helpful student she'd met.

2   **In the space provided write the superlative of the adjective in the brackets.**

a. The baby was the (fat) _____ in the competition.

b. This chocolate is (creamy) _____ .

c. The (powerful) _____ car goes too fast for our roads.

d. The cheetah is the (fast) _____ animal over a short distance.

e. Maths with Statistics is the (difficult) _____ subject in school.

3   **Using a red pen underline the comparatives and circle the superlatives in each of the following sentences.**

a. All three dogs looked pretty fat but the problem was deciding which one was the fattest. The German Shepherd was definitely fatter than the Dalmatian but was it heavier than the Great Dane?

b. What a disaster – so much for making a birthday cake for my dad. The first attempt was crumblier than a sandcastle and the second was crumblier still. The most sensible idea would have been to buy one!

ISBN: 9780170462990

VERBS

A verb is a doing word.

The verb is the doing or action word in a sentence. It needs somebody or something to be doing the action.

1 **Underline the verbs in the following sentences.**

    a. Jackson chased the ball.

    b. Bella barked at the cat.

    c. I understand you.

    d. My sister loves horses.

    e. Peter swam in the sea.

2 **Complete the sentences by putting an appropriate verb in the spaces.**

    a. Maddison _____ all her dessert.

    b. The chicken _____ in the oven.

    c. Mike _____ his bike.

    d. The cat _____ its dinner.

    e. Duncan _____ his claymore.

Verb tenses

In English, there are three basic tenses:

- **Present** (the action is happening now)
- **Past** (the action has already happened)
- **Future** (the action will happen)

1 **In the spaces provided, write down which basic tense the sentence is – present, past or future.**

    a. The toaster cooked my bread. _____

    b. I will dry the dishes after dinner. _____

    c. Daniel is unwell today. _____

    d. Tomo finished his science fair project. _____

    e. The roses bloom beautifully. _____

    f. The children will walk home from school. _____

ISBN: 9780170462990

Extension work with verbs and tenses

Within each tense, there are four tense forms (so 12 tenses in all). These are:

- Simple
- Perfect
- Continuous
- Perfect continuous.

Below is an explanation of the four forms associated with examples using the present tense:

The **simple** tense form is the most commonly used tense and is used for declarations.

For example: *Jackson is a dog. (Present simple tense form)*

The **perfect** form shows actions that happened at an indefinite time.

For example: *I have washed the car. (Present perfect tense form)*

The **continuous** form shows action happening at the moment.

For example: *I am writing my novel. (Present continuous tense form)*

The **perfect continuous** form has action that started in the past and continues in the present.

For example: *She has been tidying her room for over three hours.*
                   (Present perfect continuous tense form)

1 **In the spaces below, write down what form of the present tense the verb is written in.** *For example: 'I wash my hair every second day' is present simple.*

  a. I am flying to Australia on Saturday.   _____

  b. Dad eats two eggs for breakfast every morning. _____

  c. Someone has just stolen my wallet.   _____

  d. My dogs have been swimming in the creek.   _____

2 **In the spaces below, write down what form of the past tense the verb is written in.** *For example: 'When we got to the theatre, the movie had already started' is past perfect tense.*

  a. By the time I had watched my favourite programme, I had
      drunk a whole bottle of Coke.   _____

  b. I was texting in English when Mrs Hayes caught me. _____

  c. Jose had been cleaning out her files when she came
      across some money in an envelope.   _____

  d. Jayden attended Kaikorai Valley College as a student. _____

ISBN: 9780170462990

3 **In the spaces below, write down what form of the future tense the verb is written in.** *For example: 'How long will you have been studying Spanish by the time you finish high school?' is future perfect continuous.*

a. Sam and Mackenna will arrive home before us. _____

b. Once exams are over, we are going to be partying hard. _____

c. The principal will have retired before I finish school. _____

d. We will have been driving for nine hours by the time we get to Ōtepoti. _____

Auxiliary verbs

These are verbs that have a special job and are often called 'helping verbs' because they help the main verb by suggesting or modifying the mood or time of the verb.

There are 23 auxiliary verbs:

may	am	do	could	had	can	
might	are	does	should	has	will	
must	be	did	would	have	shall	
	being					
	been					
	is					
	was					
	were					

1 **Underline the auxiliary verb in the sentences below:**

a. Katie and Brianna may come over later.

b. Do your teeth ache when you eat ice-cream?

c. Lalei wondered if she should take her coat to school.

d. The cat has gone into the rubbish again!

e. Jess and Ben will get their badges on Friday.

f. Who did your hair? I am so jealous!

g. Can my dad borrow your dad's trailer?

h. I have not been well lately so I may not be able to help you this weekend.

i. 'You might have thought about that before you took the lid off,' Mum growled. 'Now, I will have to use it all up tonight,' she said, waving the container of seafood.

> Sometimes there will be an extra word or two between the helping verb and the main verb.
>
> A sentence may contain up to three helping verbs to the main verb.

ADVERBS

An adverb tells us how, when or where an action takes place.

Just as an ADjective ADDS more information about the noun (the naming word), an ADverb ADDS more information about the verb (the action).

These are the types of adverbs:

Adverbs of manner

Adverbs of certainty

Adverbs of place

Adverbs of degree.

Adverbs of time

Adverbs of frequency

Adverbs of comment

Adverbs of manner tell **how** someone does something.
*For example: Jack drives very **carefully**.*

1   **Underline the adverbs of manner (how) in the following sentences.**

a. The dog snored erratically.

b. The woman placed her hand gently on the baby's head.

c. Eating hot pizza fast can burn your mouth.

d. That movie went so slowly.

Adverbs of time tell us **when** something happens.
*For example: We'll let you know our decision **next week**.*

2   **Underline the adverbs of time (when) in the following sentences.**

a. I cannot believe it was only yesterday that I was promoted.

b. 'Since when are you allowed to come home after ten o'clock?' Dad demanded.

c. Before I take the dogs for a walk, I always feed them.

d. I will talk to you soon.

Adverbs of certainty tell us **how sure** someone feels about an action.
*For example: I **probably** left my phone at home.*

3   **Underline the adverbs of certainty (how sure) in the following sentences.**

a. Susan is definitely a team player.

b. He won't forget his keys again, surely.

c. Certainly, I will put your name on the list.

d. They probably thought you would pay for the tickets.

ISBN: 9780170462990

Adverbs of frequency tell us **how often** something happens.

For example: *They **usually** get to work at eight o'clock.*

4 **Underline the adverbs of frequency (how often) in the following sentences.**

a. Sometimes I would rather watch television than study.

b. Dad says I often talk in my sleep.

c. We usually go to the Farmers' Market every Saturday morning.

d. I occasionally google my name.

Adverbs of place tell us **where** something is done.

For example: *I'm going back to Scouts next year.*

5 **Underline the adverbs of place (where) in the following sentences.**

a. I couldn't find my file anywhere on my laptop.

b. Nowhere does it say I have to like you.

c. If you are going to put your gear somewhere, it might as well go here.

d. Your book is everywhere! You must be so pleased.

Adverbs of comment provide a **comment or opinion** about a situation.

For example: *Fortunately, there were enough seats left for the concert.*

6 **Underline the adverbs of comment (opinion) in the following sentences.**

a. Luckily, she had remembered to bring her EFTPOS card.

b. They deleted the series, unfortunately, because its ratings were poor.

c. I am here, happily, to give this award for your son's diligence.

d. Joshua angrily brushed away his tears.

Adverbs of degree tell us about the **intensity** of an action, adjective or another adverb.

For example: *They **hardly** use their golf clubs.*

7 **Underline the adverbs of degree (opinion) in the following sentences.**

a. I almost dropped my laptop.

b. My cat doesn't just like you – she loves you!

c. He worked extremely hard to get that Maths prize.

d. She put enough water in the vase to keep the flowers alive for a week.

CONJUNCTIONS

A conjunction is a word that joins words and sentences.

A conjunction is a joining word. There are two types of conjunctions: coordinating and subordinating. Both types have very specific roles in the sentence structure. A coordinating conjunction joins sentences that are equal in structure and importance.

For example: *I had to return the book but I hadn't finished reading it.*

Both sentences on either side of the word 'but' are main clauses and 'equal' in grammatical structure.

There are only seven coordinating conjunctions. Consider these words as the elite of joining:

for	and	nor	
but	or	yet	so

People remember these with the acronym **FANBOYS**.

The subordinating conjunction joins a subordinate clause to a main clause (sentence).

For example: *I no longer eat bread because it makes me ill.*

'I no longer eat bread' is a main clause and makes sense on its own. 'because it makes me ill' is a subordinate clause because it does not make sense on its own. It needs the main clause too. Some of the mostly commonly used examples of subordinating conjunctions are:

because	although	since	therefore	however
until	when	whenever	before	while
as	whether			

1 **Underline the** conjunctions **in the following sentences. In the spaces provided, write whether the conjunction is** coordinating **or** subordinating**.**

a. He was my teacher and my coach. _____

b. I wasn't working hard so my mother encouraged me. _____

c. You can have fried bread or some mutton bird. _____

d. Because Gran is coming to visit, you will tidy the kitchen. _____

e. I considered the idea but it was not right for us. _____

f. Dan was a great horse although his costs were high. _____

2 **Complete the sentences by using the correct** conjunction**.**

a. I am having bread _____ cheese for lunch.

b. I would have voted for him _____ he did not answer my questions.

c. You take the high road _____ I take the low road.

d. We can order Chinese _____ Thai for dinner tonight.

e. The school council took a stand _____ the Year 13s had to act.

ISBN: 9780170462990

PREPOSITIONS

A preposition is a word that tells us the position or place of something in relation to something else.

A preposition is a word that tells the reader, like an adverb, the positioning of action. Prepositions are a bit tricky because they show up in sentences very secretly.

Here is a list of the most commonly used prepositions:

above	behind	from	on	round	up
across	below	in	onto	through	upon
after	beneath	inside	opposite	to	with
against	beside	into	outside	toward	within
along	between	near	over	towards	without
amidst	beyond	of	past	under	
among	by	off	per	underneath	

1   **Underline the preposition in each of the following sentences.**

    a. She pondered on the value of her assignment.

    b. The results of Polyfest were posted on the website.

    c. My father took the carcass beyond the city limits.

    d. If you look between the schedules for the arts calendar and the drama one, you can see that there is a conflict of interest.

2   **Using the list above, put in the appropriate preposition.**

    a. I put my cup _____ the bench.

    b. The kennel was _____ the stables.

    c. The chef poured the sauce _____ the steak.

    d. They put the Christmas fairy _____ the top of the tree.

    e. Samara was seated _____ Dillan for the class photo.

3   **Read the following passage and circle all the prepositions you spot.**

I lay on my bed thinking. Tomorrow I would be in Whangārei and sitting in a meeting with other teens like me. Mum had made my lunch and poured tomato sauce onto the bread in an attempt to make me feel like it was just another school day. She was wrong because Thursday was going to be the complete opposite to any other school day.

PUNCTUATION

No one is going to take you seriously if you make mistakes with the basics of spelling and punctuation. Getting things such as capital letters, commas, apostrophes and paragraphing correct is critical if you want to communicate your written work clearly with people. Trust us when we tell you these things are important, so let's take another look at them so you get them right!

Capital letters

All proper nouns and the beginning of sentences must have a capital letter. This includes titles for books, movies, ships, shops; the names of months and days of the week; people. They all deserve their capital letter status.

1 **Rewrite the following, changing lower case letters to capital letters where necessary:**

a. ava told me she doesn't go to the coffee pot cafe because she hates coffee.

_____

b. new york city is actually the place to be if you love film and literature.

_____

c. border collies are the best breed for competitions.

_____

d. thoroughbred horses are, according to the dressage committee, too difficult for inclusion in any local competition.

_____

_____

e. agatha gates, principal of wonderful girls college, is to address the board of trustees next tuesday.

_____

_____

2 **Rewrite the following, changing lower case letters to capital letters and adding other punctuation marks where necessary:**

a. what are your family doing for waitangi weekend

_____

b. i keep saturdays and sundays for me time

_____

c. my cousin daniel has graduated from dental school

_____

d. november and december are busy months because of the lead-up to christmas

_____

e. her mum never complains about her lucky thing mum is always going on about my room

_____

Speech marks

The rule of thumb is that everything that is said MUST BE contained in the speech marks, including the punctuation that goes with it. So, if a person asks a question, the question mark is included inside the speech marks.

For example: *'How do you do that?' she asked.*

1 **Punctuate the following with speech marks.**

a. Give it to me now, the boy cried.

b. I am your friend, the old woman said.

c. Are you serious? he asked. That is a stupid thing to do.

d. English teachers are, in the main, careful and kind, the principal remarked.

e. The phone call is for you, Mum said. Don't be too long, okay?

2 **Punctuate the following with speech marks, commas and full stops to make the meaning clear.**

a. I have taken the dogs for a walk she told him but they haven't been fed yet

b. Listen I said You are going to have to trust me

c. Mrs Sharpe looked at me for a moment before speaking. You are quite mistaken she said

d. How many times do I have to tell you stop tickling me

e. Matthew wasn't listening. Hey turn off your iPod I cried listen to me

3 **You be the proof reader. The following passage has many punctuation errors. Using a red pen, correct all the mistakes you can find. (We suggest you do it in pencil first.)**

today started well enough. i had completed all my english homework during last nights episode of dr who ms swire wasnt in a mood for once even though she said im surprised that your's is the first essay in damon. by the afternoon even my mate's we're wanting to know how id done it. did you get one of your sister's to do it pete asked. ms swire mustve said something in the staff room because mr walpert even patted me on the back congratulations he said i knew you would start to improve sooner or later. i went out to dunedin riding school to ride dan my horse but he was lame so i spent the afternoon picking up bag's of horse manure. by the time id arrived back home i was tired, stinking but id made ten buck's the days strange school experience a fading memory until i unpacked my bag this time it was mr walperts class assignment due tomorrow thank goodness tonights telly highlight was a re-run of captain amazing although i hope mr walpert wouldnt react the same as my english teacher

DIRECT AND REPORTED SPEECH

Direct speech means the exact words that someone has spoken and they are shown by speech marks ' '.

For example: *'I don't want to go shopping,' Melissa cried.*

Reported speech is when what has been said is told to the reader (is reported). There are no speech marks around reported speech.

For example: *Melissa said she did not want to go shopping.*

1   **Read the following sentences carefully and in the space provided write either 'reported' or 'direct'.**

a.   I told him that he couldn't have any more dessert.   _____

b.   'Stop! Your feet are wet,' his mother called.   _____

c.   'Take this form to the office please,' the teacher said.   _____

d.   She told me to take the form to the office.   _____

e.   I said that they were not to do it yet.   _____

There are two main rules you need to obey when you change **direct speech** into **reported speech**:

1   You must change the tense of the verbs from present tense to past tense, for example *'**I have** just eaten my dinner'* to ***She had** just eaten her dinner.*

2   You must change the personal pronouns into third person pronouns, for example *'**I have** just eaten my dinner'* to ***She had** just eaten her dinner.*

2   **The following sentences are all direct speech. Rewrite them in reported speech.**

a.   'We'll have to turn around and go back the way we came,' sighed Mrs Harvey.

_____

_____

b.   'It's gonna be tight. Go as far right as you can and then reverse back,' Sophie called.

_____

_____

_____

c.   'I really wish I'd remembered that map,' the older woman muttered.

_____

_____

_____

ISBN: 9780170462990

d. 'I know this bush really well. I've got secret spots.' Malcolm turned to her and smiled. 'I bring the babes up here.'

_____

_____

_____

e. 'We had to lock our parrot up because he kept eating the tea towels,' Jo said to Carlie. 'Is he mad?' Carlie asked. 'Well, he certainly isn't pleased,' Jo replied.

_____

_____

_____

_____

_____

> When changing **reported speech** into **direct speech**, remember to give a new paragraph every time someone new begins to speak.

3 **The following sentences are all reported speech. Rewrite them in direct speech.**

a. The constable detained the young boy and asked him what his name was, where he lived, and what he was doing sneaking around the back of the shop. The boy told him that he didn't know the answers to any of the questions.

_____

_____

_____

_____

_____

b. The Prime Minister announced today that all teenagers would receive an allowance of $15 per week. When asked by a parent how the government would fund the extra cost, the Prime Minister replied that she would take it out of the pay packets of the parents.

_____

_____

_____

_____

_____

_____

QUESTION AND EXCLAMATION MARKS

Think back to when you learnt about full stops. Do you remember that they mark the end of a sentence? Well, a question mark and an exclamation mark do the same job. They are both found at the end of a sentence but they indicate the **tone** of the sentence to the reader.

Question marks

A question mark is used at the end of a sentence that asks a direct question.

When you ask a direct question the sentence ends with a question mark rather than a full stop.
For example: *'Do you understand the definition?'*

However, when a sentence does not contain a direct question but only a reported one, the sentence ends with a full stop, not a question mark.
For example: *'Matiu asked me if I wanted to go to Te Matatini.'*

This is a reported question — the question is not directly asked to the person so does not have a question mark. If it had read 'Do you want to go to the beach?', then we would place a question mark at the end of the sentence as it was spoken directly to a person.

1 Test your skills at identifying a reported or direct question. Read the following sentences carefully and in the space provided write either reported or direct.

   a. Would you like a drink with your dinner, sir? _____

   b. The first question he asked me was what was my address. _____

   c. Did you go to watch the fireworks? _____

   d. Carmel asked me if I would like to go and have coffee. _____

   e. How much does that pounamu cost? _____

2 Place a full stop or a question mark where appropriate.

   a. The sky is very blue today _____

   b. Did the All Blacks win their game last night _____

   c. Will you be attending the opening night of the
       Stage Challenge _____

   d. The first thing we did was ask if Lucy was all right _____

   e. Georgia, look at the trees blowing in the wind _____

ISBN: 9780170462990

3 **There are too many question marks in the following passages. Put a line through those that are unnecessary.**

a. Will you be going to Mark and Jacqui's wedding? It is going to be wonderful. Are you planning to fly? We are going to leave on the Tuesday and return on the Sunday. Apparently we've been asked to help with the flowers?

b. Wow. Wasn't that movie great? Talk about a roller coaster ride? Isn't Liam Hemsworth a spunk? Lexi asked if he was in the *Avengers* movie but I thought it was his brother? Do you know?

c. I was asked to join the Wednesday Kapa Haka group? Do you think it is a good idea? I'm not sure what to think?

Exclamation marks

An exclamation mark is used at the end of a sentence that shows strong feeling.

Exclamatory sentences are usually short and are most often used in direct speech (this is when the speaker's exact words are given). Like the question mark, it helps the reader to understand the way the sentence would be read.

For example: 'Good grief!', 'What do you think you are doing?!'

Avoid overusing the exclamation mark in your writing. You should only use an exclamation mark when someone shouts, cries out, gives an order or says something forcefully. It is designed for dramatic effect, not humour, and if you overuse it, it will lose its impact.

 1 **Rewrite the following sentences, putting in the full stops, capital letters and exclamation marks.**

a. get off the carpet in your muddy gumboots now

_____

b. help the waka is sinking

_____

c. ouch ouch that stupid hammer

_____

d. take that you swine

_____

e. hooray, I passed my science exam

_____

2 **There are too many exclamation marks in the following passages. Put a line through those that are unnecessary.**

a. I can't believe it! The Manumia Memorial Trophy is ours! Didn't the team do a brilliant job? I've had an awesome day at Polyfest! I can't wait until next year when we can do it all again!

b. Run for your life! The lions have escaped their enclosure and are heading this way! We have to get to the four-wheel-drive! It's this way, behind that tent! Quick!

c. 'Would you like to come to my brother's birthday bash? It will be a rage! The best party on earth!'
'Absolutely! I wouldn't miss it for the world! Are you inviting Matti and Jack? I wonder if Jess will be there. What a babe!'

Putting them all together

1 **Place a full stop, question mark or exclamation mark at the end of the following sentences.**

a. How many subjects are you taking this year _____

b. Get out of here. Now _____

c. What do you think you are doing, young lady _____

d. I loved the latest Taika Waititi movie _____

e. Wow, I can't believe it _____

f. Do you remember what time the bus is leaving _____

g. We need to get to the bank by four o'clock _____

h. Who owns this sweatshirt _____

i. Greer asked me if I wanted her to pick me up or to meet her at the party _____

j. Hoane shouted, 'Look at this _____ Look at this _____ '

ISBN: 9780170462990   PHOTOCOPYING OF THIS PAGE IS RESTRICTED UNDER LAW.

COLONS AND SEMI-COLONS

Colons and semi-colons are closely related and you may get them a little confused. Unlike the exclamation and question marks, a colon and a semi-colon are not used instead of a full stop. They are used in the middle of sentences and have a similar use to that of a comma or conjunction.

Colons

The colon (:) introduces more information or shows divisions.

There are several uses for a colon:

- To introduce a list of things or people.

  For example: *You will need the following for Year 10 English: 1B5 workbook, jotter pad, refill, clear file.*

- Used between two clauses when the second one explains or gives more information about the first.

  For example: *Stop right there: your feet are filthy.*

- To introduce quotations or speeches in scripts.

  For example: *Lady Macbeth: Out, damned spot ...*

- To show divisions of time, parts of the Bible and play references.

  For example: *Time — 1:30 pm, 5:00 am*
  Bible — Exodus 23: 1–8 (Book of Exodus, chapter 28, verses 1–8)
  Play reference — Hamlet, 3:2 (Hamlet, Act 3, Scene 2).

1 **Using a red pen, punctuate the following sentences with colons.**

a. You will need to bring the following items scissors, 20 cm ruler, 3B pencil, craft glue, craft knife, assorted coloured paper.

b. I need to get these things from the supermarket butter, toilet paper, dog roll, baby rice.

c. At 830 on Saturday morning, Riley goes to swimming.

d. The places we will visit are as follows Christchurch, Wanaka, Queenstown, Te Anau, Milford, Dunedin.

e. Please send the following ASAP passport, Visa card, address book, cellphone.

f. In English this year we did a close reading of Act 5 4 from *Romeo and Juliet* and then watched the corresponding section of the film.

ISBN: 9780170462990

Semi-colons

A semi-colon (;) is used to break up long sentences and lists or join clauses that are closely related.

There are two main uses for a semi-colon:

- to join sentences when there is no conjunction
- to mark off items in a complicated list, especially one that already contains commas.

Semi-colons can be confusing, so let's explain each of these uses in more detail.

We know from previous exercises that a conjunction joins together two sentences/clauses. Sometimes it is possible to use a semi-colon to replace a coordinating conjunction.

For example:

My dog loves milk and my cat loves water.

My dog loves milk; my cat loves water.

The second use is to separate a complicated list, usually statements that will make sense on their own but are about the same subject.

For example:

I enjoy my cat: she doesn't talk back; she cleans herself; she feeds herself; and she is nice to cuddle.

The most common place you will see the semi-colon in use is in the dictionary. Look at how the semi-colon helps to divide the following definition:

Sky *n* the apparent canopy over our heads; the heavens; the weather; the upper rows of pictures in a gallery.

1 **Using a red pen, punctuate the following sentences with semi-colons.**

   a. You own the dog you walk the dog.

   b. I enjoy standing in cowpats my dad thinks it's disgusting!

   c. I like my bad memory: I forget my mistakes I forget other people's mistakes I can watch the same movie again and again.

   d. Jennifer struggles with Maths she succeeds at English.

   e. How to make toast: cook the bread butter the toast eat the toast.

   f. **length** *n* quality of being long extent from end to end the longest measure of anything.

ISBN: 9780170462990

APOSTROPHES

The apostrophe (') has two main purposes:
- to show ownership
- to show where one or more letters is missed out. These are called 'contractions'.

However, it is also used for the plurals of numbers, letters, and abbreviations.

1   **To show ownership.**
Ask yourself, 'Who is the owner?', and using a red pen, write in the apostrophe and 's'.

   a.   Mum car got broken into.
   b.   I could not take my eyes from the teacher frown.
   c.   Michelle and Marcel parents come from France.
   d.   My mother and father clothes are so out of style!
   e.   Donna cats bowls are always dirty. That is what you get with five cats.

> If the word does not end in s, add an apostrophe + s = 's.
> *The* **man's** *tie was crooked.*
> (man + 's = man's)
>
> If the word does end in s, add an apostrophe after the s.
> *Our three* **cats'** *bowls were full.*
> (cats + ' = cats')

2   **To show where one or more letters is missed out.**
Using a red pen, write in the apostrophes.

   a.   Im not supposed to eat peanuts.
   b.   Your dad says youre to go to soccer practice after school.
   c.   Dont you think youve watched too much television?
   d.   Hes a great guitar player. Youd like him.
   e.   Theyd finished the pancakes before I had time to make more batter.

3   **For plurals of numbers, letters, and abbreviations.**
Using a red pen, write in the apostrophes.

   a.   Jessica scored five 10s in her gymnastic round.
   b.   The place where the helicopter landed was marked by two large Hs.
   c.   Mum told me she was tired of hearing all the 'I cants'.
   d.   The ticket officers checked all the students' IDs.
   e.   The dean warned me to mind my ps and qs.

Let's see how well you have learned when to use an apostrophe, whether it is to show ownership, a missing letter or for plurals of numbers, letters and abbreviations.

4   **In the spaces provided, rewrite the following with the correct punctuation:**

   a.   My sisters are mean to me because they wont let me play on their iPads.

   _____

   b.   The banks manager said the money boxes were our's for the taking.

   _____

   c.   Youre supposed to take Nicks bike as well as yours.

   _____

   d.   My mums muffins are the best of all the mums recipes.

   _____

ISBN: 9780170462990

BRACKETS

Brackets are most commonly used to include extra information within a sentence.

We use brackets to enclose words that give extra information or make the meaning of the sentence clearer. The rest of the sentence should still make complete sense if the words inside the brackets are taken away.

For example: *If you take away my leisure time (or anything else I like doing) I will become unhappy.*

The words in the brackets are additional information and are not absolutely necessary.

Other common uses of brackets are to:
- enclose asides
- give reference information, for example page numbers, diagrams
- indicate stage directions in scripts.

1   **Mark the following sentences with a ✓ or a ✗ to show whether** brackets **have been used correctly or not.**

a. Our new car has ABS (anti-lock braking system). ☐

b. The satellite made a close pass of the earth and took a series of images (below) of Antarctica. ☐

c. The (Beehive) and Parliament Buildings are in the centre of Wellington city. ☐

d. A semi-colon can be used instead of a conjunction (for example, 'and', 'but') to join two sentences together. ☐

e. This is my first day as a relief teacher. I have been in (a variety of subjects) for example Maths, Art and Geography. ☐

2   **Using a red pen, place** brackets **in the appropriate places.**

a. George Orwell real name Eric Blair was born in Motihari, India in 1903.

b. Rain and meltwater is then carried down the Waimakariri River, finding its way into aquifers of various depths see diagram page 67.

c. *Star Wars: The Force Awakens* also known as *Star Wars: Episode VII – The Force Awakens* is a 2015 American epic space opera film directed by J.J. Abrams.

d. There are two teams in an organised debate: they are the affirmative for and the negative against.

e. Lisa: *standing with one leg raised and a finger on nose* I can't stay like this forever you know!

ISBN: 9780170462990   PHOTOCOPYING OF THIS PAGE IS RESTRICTED UNDER LAW.

HYPHENS

Hyphens are used to join two or more words to make a compound word and to divide words at the end of a line.

The first use of a hyphen is to create compound words. These are words that are made up of two or more parts to create a new word.

For example: *I had coffee with my mother-in-law on Wednesday.*

Hyphens are also used when writing compound numbers.

For example: *She wrote the number twenty-three in the margin.*

Note: there is no space between the hyphen and the word(s) it joins.

1 **Rewrite the following words, placing the hyphens in the correct position.**

    a. parttime   _____

    b. selfrespect   _____

    c. selfaddressed   _____

    d. infrared   _____

    e. exwife   _____

The second way we use a hyphen is to divide words at the end of a line. There are times in your writing where you have room for only part of a word. A hyphen is used to split the word, signaling to the reader that the remainder of the word is carried on to the next line. You must always divide words between syllables and ensure that each part can be properly pronounced.

For example, the word *important* can be divided *im-portant* or *import-ant* but never *impo-rtant*.

2 **Mark the following words with a ✓ or a ✗ to show whether hyphens have been used correctly or not.**

a. comm-unicate ☐	**b.** butt-er ☐	**c.** refer-ences ☐
d. par-ticular ☐	**e.** re-cord ☐	**f.** tee-nager ☐
g. quali-fication ☐	**h.** anthro-pology ☐	**i.** sus-picion ☐

3 **Rewrite the following words, using a hyphen to divide the word in the best place.**

    a. wheelbarrow _____   **b.** explanation _____

    c. suddenly _____   **d.** remember _____

    e. dictionary _____   **f.** quotation _____

ISBN: 9780170462990

DASHES

The dash has three main purposes:
- **to indicate a sudden change of thought**
- **to lead to the unexpected**
- **parenthesis (give extra information).**

The dash is often used wrongly. So:
- never use a dash to replace the correct use of a comma
- never use a dash instead of a full stop
- never use a dash unless it is absolutely necessary.

1 **Rewrite the following sentences, placing dashes in the appropriate places.**

a. I bought a beautiful ring it looks good on my pig.

_____

b. When you are down, look up people like to look at your face.

_____

c. She said and she's always right that dashes are often used incorrectly.

_____

d. My brother the one with the long hair plays in a rock band.

_____

The dash may also be used:
- to mark an afterthought
- to separate a repetition
- to mark an incomplete or interrupted sentence
- to introduce or follow a list.

2 **Rewrite the following sentences, placing dashes in the appropriate places.**

a. I had a good day today it was the weekend.

_____

b. The congregation said the prayer: You are mighty, O Lord O Lord.

_____

c. 'The reason I was late look at me.'

_____

d. Native trees kauri, rimu, rātā, tītoki will be planted in the forest.

_____

ISBN: 9780170462990

RUN-ON SENTENCES

A run-on sentence is a group of sentences that 'run' together because they have not been punctuated correctly.

In *English Basics* you learned how to identify simple and compound sentences and how to correctly use full stops and capital letters and, in this book, you have learned about the colon and semi-colon. However, many people still ignore the rules for making sentences and end up with what we call 'run-on sentences'. Here is an example of a run-on sentence:

The dog trotted down the driveway it stopped at the letterbox.

It should read *The dog trotted down the driveway **and** stopped at the letterbox.*

or *The dog trotted down the driveway. It stopped at the letterbox.*

or *The dog trotted down the driveway; it stopped at the letterbox.*

1 **Using a red pen correct the following run-on sentences by placing full stops and capital letters where appropriate.**

   a. The rain had ceased at last leaves glistened as the wind played with them.

   b. I went to the beach it was very windy and I lost my hat darn it!

   c. The riders revved their engines the noise was deafening the flag dropped and they were off.

   d. That is disgusting you wouldn't catch me eating any of the things they make them eat on *Survivor* they must be desperate!

   e. It is essential that young people learn to eat properly childhood obesity is becoming a major problem world-wide it must be stopped.

2 **Using a red pen, correct the run-on sentences in this passage:**

   The whole class waited, Ms Donovan had asked twice already and no one was leaving until the truth was out so they waited not one person was brave enough to spill the beans, not even Megan, their teacher stood at the front of the room with her hands on her hips, staring at them, all of them.

Using sentences effectively

You have learnt about simple and compound sentences but there are other forms of sentences that you can learn about. When you edit your work, you can then use a variety of sentence types to avoid run-on sentences and this will also make your writing more interesting. The next few pages will teach you to recognise and utilise them. It is tricky stuff, so take your time and ask questions if you need to.

MINOR SENTENCES

A minor sentence is a group of words that do not make sense on their own. It needs a simple sentence to make it complete. There are two main types of minor sentences: the phrase and the subordinate clause.

The phrase

A phrase is a group of words without a verb.

For example: *Behind the red chair*
                    In my mother's car
                    Before my shower

None of the above makes sense just on its own. We need to add a simple sentence to complete the whole thing.

For example: *Behind the red chair*, my book was against the wall.
                    In my mother's car, my brother waited for me.
                    I want to eat breakfast *before my shower*.

 Underline the phrases in the following sentences:

    a. I stayed with my grandmother during the holidays.

    b. He ran around the yard like a chook without its head.

    c. A few hours later the teenagers went swimming.

    d. I saw the bright light down the end of the tunnel.

    e. Lyle quietly closed the door after arriving late.

There are three main types of phrase and each does the job of giving a more interesting description to your writing.

Adjectival phrase
Remember that an adjective describes the noun, so an adjectival phrase is a group of words whose job it is to describe the noun.
For example: *My brother,* ***strange and kooky****, left the room.*

Adverbial phrase
Remember that an adverb describes the how, where or when of the verb, so an adverbial phrase is a group of words whose job it is to describe the verb.
For example: ***Stretching carefully and with discomfort****, he flexed his muscles.*

Noun phrase
A noun phrase gives more information about a place, person or thing.
For example: *This is my father,* ***Chairman of the Board of Trustees****.*

ISBN: 9780170462990

2 **Beside each sentence, write what type of phrase is in italics.**

a. *Without raising my voice,* I called the children to me. _____

b. I instructed the child to sit *over by the window next to Sammy.* _____

c. The *condemned holiday* bach belonged to the old woman. _____

d. The cat, *exhausted from her mouse hunt,* went straight to sleep. _____

e. My teacher, *nervous and pale,* began to call the roll. _____

3 **Rewrite the following sentences, adding phrases to make the sentences more interesting. You could do all adjectival phrases first, then, on a separate sheet of paper, redo them with adverbial phrases and finally with noun phrases.**

a. I popped the pimple on my cheek.

_____

b. The waves crashed onto the beach.

_____

c. I was embarrassed to sit beside Shannon.

_____

d. The woman pulled closed the curtains.

_____

e. The dog howled.

_____

The subordinate clause

Sometimes, a sentence does have a verb but it still does not make sense on its own, for example: 'Before I wash my hair.' This is called a **subordinate clause**; 'subordinate' means something or someone lower than something or someone else, like a private in the army is subordinate to a sergeant. These subordinate clauses also need a simple sentence to complete the meaning.

1 **Underline the subordinate clauses in the following sentences.**

a. I will take a sandwich after you have chosen one.

b. Tāmaki Makaurau is a New Zealand city which has the most people in it.

c. He knew the best songs which made everyone happy.

d. This is my cousin who came first in the Manu Kōrero speech contest.

e. Unless I study I won't pass the exams.

2 **In the space provided, write down phrase or subordinate clause for the words in italics.**

a. My team is working hard *because it needs to.* _____

b. *Yesterday afternoon,* I watched The Black Ferns win again. _____

c. The cricketer, *with a long history of success,* spoke at assembly. _____

d. You must beat the eggs, *after you whip the cream.* _____

e. His eyes followed the bus, *a disappearing spot on the horizon.* _____

SIMPLE AND COMPOUND SENTENCES

Simple sentences

A simple sentence is a name for a sentence that can make complete sense from the beginning to the full stop. It must contain a **subject** (a thing or person who does the action) and a **verb** (action). It often will have an **object** (but does not have to). Another name for a simple sentence is 'main clause' or 'interdependent clause'.

Here is an example of a simple sentence:

I *(the subject)* **sang** *(the verb)* **a song** *(the object).*

or

I *(the subject)* **sang** *(the verb).*

A simple sentence is like a train engine in that, with the driver (the subject) and engine (the verb), it can move along the tracks independently.

However, sometimes the subject in a sentence is not included but the sentence is STILL called a simple sentence (or independent clause) because it is still complete. That's because, especially when we talk to each other, we sometimes leave out the subject but it is still implied:

For example: *Take it!*

Because the subject 'you' or someone's name, is implied, this is a simple sentence.

1 **Look carefully at the following sentences and show whether they are minor sentences (independent clauses) by circling either YES or NO.**

a.	Bella went for a run.	YES NO
b.	Yesterday.	YES NO
c.	It hasn't finished.	YES NO
d.	Don't touch that!	YES NO
e.	At the back of the house.	YES NO
f.	Swung it out wide.	YES NO
g.	The mangy looking cat hid underneath the cluttered stairwell.	YES NO

ISBN: 9780170462990

Compound sentences

A compound sentence is the name for a sentence that contains two or more simple sentences (independent clauses) joined by coordinating conjunctions. Remember these are:

for	and	nor	so
but	or	yet	

For example:

> Phillip sat on the couch   *and*   Dallas sat at the table.
>   [simple sentence]   [coordinating conjunction]   [simple sentence]

A compound sentence is like two or more train engines joined. They are more powerful than just one – just as your writing can provide more information instead of using only simple sentences.

1   **Using a coordinating conjunction, turn the following into** compound sentences**:**

a. Miles scored. The game was won.

_____

b. I want to hear the television. Stop chewing.

_____

c. Rauhina had eggs for breakfast. Justin had toast.

_____

d. Jessica went to Otago. Niall stayed in Dunedin. Josh went to Auckland.

_____

e. Minstrel was lame. Purdie was too old. Katie rode Willow.

_____

f. The weather had turned bad. The picnic was cancelled.

_____

g. Finished all my homework. Time for computer games.

_____

COMPLEX SENTENCES

The complex sentence is one simple sentence joined to one or more subordinating clauses.

It is joined with a conjunction (a joining word) or separated by a semi-colon or comma.

For example:

    I ate my pie quickly   *without*   *dropping my knife or fork.*
      [simple sentence]   *[conjunction]*   *[subordinating clause]*

If we wrote in simple or compound sentences all the time, our writing would get very boring. We use complex sentences to link ideas and images together and to add information to our main points.

A complex sentence is the same as an engine and carriages joined. Just as it is interesting to watch a train go by and look at the different carriages it is pulling, our writing creates more interest with these extra attachments to our sentences.

And, don't forget: sometimes a train engine will push a carriage, sometimes it will pull a carriage and sometimes it will do both. It is the same with a complex sentence: sometimes, the simple sentence is at the start; sometimes it is at the end; and sometimes it is in the middle.

1   **Underline the simple sentence in the following complex sentences:**

    a.   When he fell over, my brother broke his finger.

    b.   I love my car; especially when I wash it.

    c.   Homework, when done regularly, can help me understand my schoolwork.

    d.   Putting a hand on his son's shoulder, Tom pushed him away.

    e.   The elderly woman brought the hankie to her mouth, coughing harshly.

2   **Add a conjunction and a minor sentence to the following simple sentences to make a complex sentence.**

    a.   I bought the groceries at the supermarket _____

        _____

    b.   _____

        _____ on Fridays I go to the movies.

    c.   My father rides his mountain bike down at the beach _____

        _____

d. _____

_____ I pulled on my running shoes.

e. School is such a social place _____

_____

3   **Write down a complex sentence from the following paragraph:**

> When Sophie brought her hand back into the light of the torch to check it, she was disgusted to see it covered in blood. Quickly she shone the torch down and her worst fears were realised. Oh no! Mrs Harvey was going nowhere in a huge hurry with that leg.

_____

_____

4   **Finish the following to make them into complex sentences.**

a. Under the scorching sun _____

_____

b. I can't wear my school shoes _____

_____

c. Grinning like a cat _____

_____

d. My favourite show is _The Big Bang Theory_ _____

_____

e. He had just finished _____

_____

5   **Write down your own complex sentences.**

a. _____

b. _____

c. _____

d. _____

e. _____

COMPOUND-COMPLEX SENTENCES

The compound-complex sentence is two or more complex sentences joined by 'for', 'and', 'nor', 'but', 'or', 'yet', 'so' or a semi-colon.

For example: *The students burst out laughing without being prompted and when they had finished, they smiled for the rest of the performance.*

Broken down into sections, it looks like this:

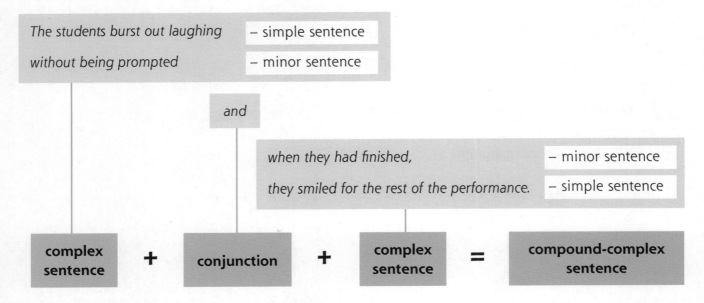

| *The students burst out laughing* | – simple sentence |
| *without being prompted* | – minor sentence |

and

| *when they had finished,* | – minor sentence |
| *they smiled for the rest of the performance.* | – simple sentence |

complex sentence **+** **conjunction** **+** **complex sentence** **=** **compound-complex sentence**

These very long sentences are used for variety in our writing. We need to take care that we don't use these types of sentences too often or our writing can become long-winded. However, they are good sentences to use with the other types.

Sometimes you will see a train which has more than one engine and many, many carriages. This is usually because they are transporting large quantities of goods or equipment. Compound-complex sentences work in a similar way: they 'carry' or 'transport' a lot of extra information.

 Read the following extract and underline the compound-complex sentence.

They could hear the music as soon as Justin stopped the car. It boomed out from the darkness, its source a bright square of light that turned out to be the Booths' garage yet people were outside, mainly huddled in little groups. Everyone was dressed warmly, for the air was chilly.

ISBN: 9780170462990

ANSWERS

(This four-page section can be removed from the centre of the book.)

PART ONE: MORE PARTS OF SPEECH pages 2-11

Nouns and Pronouns pages 2-3
Nouns
1   **a** collective   **b** common
   c proper   **d** common
   e common   **f** abstract
   g proper   **h** collective

Pronouns
Rīpeka and Riley strolled down the dirt track to the bottom of the farm. **They** were planning on having a dip in the river. Rīpeka liked to use the tyre swing. **She** would swing out and land with an almighty splash in the river.
'**You** are such a chicken Riley. **You** would love **it** if **you** just gave **it** a go.'
'No way! Last week Lucas tried **it**, missed the jump and **he** ended up hitting the tree.'
'**I** saw **him** do that! **It** was hilarious! Why don't **we** give it a go today while no one is around and **I** will show **you** how to do **it**?'
Rīpeka said. 'OK, **I** will do **it** once. **You** better promise **me** that nothing will happen or **you** are in for **it**,' Riley said.
'**I** promise **I** will look after **us**. **You** have absolutely nothing to fear.'

Possessive pronouns
1   **a** their   **b** her   **c** my, yours
   d its, its   **e** mine
2 *Our suggestion:* I always believed that **I** would be a singer. My auntie told **me** that **I** must persevere and practise every day. She was a famous singer and always told **her** family all about the things she did and **we** believed her.

Adjectives page 4
1 **a** awesome   **b** blank
   c warm, soft   **d** sleek
   e crunching
2 tired/exhausted   starving/hungry
   small/minuscule   hideous/ugly
   good/fantastic   gorgeous/pretty
   surprising/astounding   enormous/big
   hot/boiling   ancient/old
   dirty/filthy   furious/angry
   clean/spotless   hysterical/funny
3 Parent/guardian/teacher to check.

Comparatives page 5
1 **a** smaller   **b** bluer
   c more important   **d** more relaxed
   e crazier, more helpful
2 **a** paler   **b** nicer
   c slower   **d** cleaner
   e more uncomfortable
   f more interesting   **g** stricter
   h more difficult
   i more complicated
   j smoother   **k** faster
   l easier

Superlatives page 6
1 **a** juiciest   **b** stupidest
   c most favourite   **d** worst
   e most helpful
2 **a** fattest   **b** creamiest
   c most powerful   **d** fastest
   e most difficult
3 **a** Comparatives: fatter, heavier
    Superlative: fattest

b Comparative: crumblier
   Superlative: most sensible

Verbs pages 7-9
1 **a** chased   **b** barked
   c understand   **d** loves
   e swam
2 *Our suggestions:*
   a ate   **b** roasted
   c pedalled   **d** chewed
   e wielded

Verb tenses
a Past   **b** Future
c Present   **d** Past
e Present   **f** Future

Extension work with verbs and tenses
1 **a** present continuous
   b present simple
   c present perfect
   d present perfect continuous
2 **a** past perfect
   b past continuous
   c past perfect continuous
   d past simple
3 **a** future simple
   b future continuous
   c future perfect
   d future perfect continuous

Auxiliary verbs
1 **a** may   **b** Do
   c should   **d** has
   e will   **f** did, am
   g Can
   h have, been, may, be
   i might, have, will, have

Adverbs page 10
1 **a** erratically   **b** gently
   c fast   **d** slowly
2 **a** yesterday   **b** Since when
   c Before   **d** soon
3 **a** definitely   **b** surely
   c Certainly   **d** probably
4 **a** Sometimes   **b** often
   c usually   **d** occasionally
5 **a** anywhere   **b** Nowhere
   c somewhere   **d** everywhere
6 **a** Luckily   **b** unfortunately
   c happily   **d** angrily
7 **a** almost   **b** just
   c extremely   **d** too

PART TWO: MORE PUNCTUATION AND GRAMMAR pages 12-26

Conjunctions page 12
1 **a** and/coordinating
   b so/coordinating
   c or/coordinating
   d Because/subordinating
   e but/coordinating
   f although/subordinating
2 *Our suggestions:*
   a and   **b** but   **c** and   **d** or   **e** so

Prepositions page 13
1 **a** on   **b** on
   c beyond   **d** between
2 *Our suggestions:*
   a on   **b** behind
   c over   **d** on
   e beside

3 on, in, in, with, onto, in

Capital letters page 14
1 **a** Ava told me she doesn't go to the Coffee Pot Cafe because she hates coffee.
   b New York City is actually the place to be if you love film and literature.
   c Border Collies are the best breed for competitions.
   d Thoroughbred horses are, according to the Dressage Committee, too difficult for inclusion in any local competition.
   e Agatha Gates, principal of Wonderful Girls College, is to address the Board of Trustees next Tuesday.
2 **a** What are your family doing for Waitangi Weekend?
   b I keep Saturdays and Sundays for me time.
   c My cousin Daniel has graduated from Dental School.
   d November and December are busy months because of the lead-up to Christmas.
   e Her mum never complains about her. Lucky thing. Mum is always going on about my room.

Speech marks page 15
1 **a** 'Give it to me now,' the boy cried.
   b 'I am your friend,' the old woman said.
   c 'Are you serious?' he asked. 'That is a stupid thing to do.'
   d 'English teachers are, in the main, careful and kind,' the principal remarked.
   e 'The phone call is for you,' Mum said. 'Don't be too long, okay?'
2 **a** 'I have taken the dogs for a walk,' she told him, 'but they haven't been fed yet.'
   b 'Listen!' I said. 'You are going to have to trust me.'
   c Mrs Sharpe looked at me for a moment before speaking. 'You are quite mistaken,' she said.
   d 'How many times do I have to tell you? Stop tickling me.'
   e Matthew wasn't listening. 'Hey. Turn off your iPod,' I cried. 'Listen to me.'
3 Today started well enough. I had completed all my English homework during last night's episode of 'Dr. Who'. Ms Swire wasn't in a mood for once even though she said, 'I'm surprised that yours is the first essay in, Damon.' By the afternoon, even my mates were wanting to know how I'd done it.
'Did you get one of your sisters to do it?' Pete asked.
Ms Swire must've said something in the staff room because Mr. Walpert even patted me on the back. 'Congratulations,' he said. 'I knew you would start to improve sooner or later.' I went out to Dunedin Riding School to ride Dan, my horse, but he was lame so I spent the afternoon picking up bags of horse manure.
By the time I'd arrived back home, I was tired, stinking but I'd made ten bucks; the day's strange school experience a fading memory until I unpacked my bag. This time it was Mr Walpert's class

assignment due tomorrow. Thank goodness tonight's telly highlight was a re-run of 'Captain Amazing' although I hoped Mr Walpert wouldn't react the same as my English teacher.

Direct and reported speech
page 16
1 a reported **b** direct **c** direct **d** reported **e** reported
2, 3 Parent/guardian/teacher to mark.

Question marks pages 18-19
1 a direct **b** reported **c** direct **d** reported **e** direct
2 a The sky is very blue today.
b Did the All Blacks win their game last night?
c Will you be attending the opening night of the Stage Challenge?
d The first thing we did was ask if Lucy was all right.
e Georgia, look at the trees blowing in the wind.
3 a Will you be going to Mark and Jacqui's wedding? It is going to be wonderful. Are you planning to fly? We are going to leave on the Tuesday and return on the Sunday. Apparently we've been asked to help with the flowers.
b Wow. Wasn't that movie great? Talk about a roller coaster ride. Isn't Liam Hemsworth a spunk? Lexi asked if he was in the *Avengers* movies but I thought it was his brother. Do you know?
c I was asked to join the Wednesday Kapa Haka group. Do you think it is a good idea? I'm not sure what to think.

Exclamation marks pages 19-20
1 a Get off the carpet in your muddy gumboots now!
b Help! The waka is sinking.
c Ouch! Ouch! That stupid hammer.
d Take that, you swine!
e Hooray! I passed my science exam.
2 a I can't believe it! The Manumia Memorial Trophy is ours! Didn't the team do a brilliant job? I've had an awesome day at Polyfest. I can't wait until next year when we can do it all again!
b Run for your life! The lions have escaped their enclosure and are heading this way. We have to get to the four-wheel-drive. It's this way, behind that tent. Quick!
c 'Would you like to come to my brother's bash? It will be a rage. The best party on earth!' 'Absolutely! I wouldn't miss it for the world. Are you inviting Matti and Jack? I wonder if Jess will be there? What a babe!'

Putting them all together
page 20
1 a ? **b** ! **c** ? **d** . **e** !
f ? **g** . **h** ? **i** . **j** !, !

Colons page 21
a You will need to bring the following items: scissors, 20 cm ruler, 3B pencil, craft glue, craft knife, assorted coloured paper.
b I need to get these things from the supermarket: butter, toilet paper, dog roll, baby rice.
c At 8:30 a.m. on Saturday, Riley goes to swimming lessons.

d The places we will visit are as follows: Christchurch, Wanaka, Queenstown, Te Anau, Milford, Dunedin.
e Please send the following ASAP: passport, Visa card, address book, cellphone.
f In English this year we did a close reading of Act 5:4 from *Romeo and Juliet* and then watched the corresponding section of the film.

Semi-colons page 22
1 a You own the dog; you walk the dog.
b I enjoy standing in cowpats; my dad thinks it's disgusting!
c I like my bad memory: I forget my mistakes; I forget other people's mistakes; I can watch the same movie again and again.
d Jennifer struggles with Maths; she succeeds at English.
e How to make toast: cook the bread; butter the toast; eat the toast.
f **length** *n* quality of being long; extent from end to end; the longest measure of anything.

Apostrophes page 23
1 a Mum's **b** teacher's
c Michelle and Marcel's
d mother's, father's **e** Donna's cats'
2 a I'm **b** you're
c Don't, you've **d** He's, You'd
e They'd
3 a 10's **b** H's
c can't's **d** students' ID's
e p's and q's
4 a My sisters are mean to me because they won't let me play on their iPad's.
b The bank's manager said the money boxes were ours for the taking.
c You're supposed to take Nick's bike as well as yours.
d My mum's muffins are the best of all the mums' recipes.

Brackets page 24
1 a ✓ **b** ✓ **c** ✗ **d** ✓ **e** ✗
2 a George Orwell (real name Eric Blair was born in Motihari, India in 1903.
b Rain and meltwater is then carried down the Waimakariri River, finding its way into aquifers of various depths (see diagram page 67).
c *Star Wars: The Force Awakens* (also known as *Star Wars: Episode VII – The Force Awakens*) is a 2015 American epic space opera film directed by J.J. Abrams.
d There are two teams in an organised debate: they are the affirmative (for) and the negative (against).
e Lisa: (*standing with one leg raised and a finger on nose*) I can't stay like this forever you know!

Hyphens page 25
1 a part-time **b** self-respect
c self-addressed **d** infra-red
e ex-wife
2 a ✗ **b** ✗ **c** ✓ **d** ✓ **e** ✓
f ✗ **g** ✓ **h** ✓ **i** ✓
3 Possible places of recommended hyphenation are indicated by the hyphen but the word must only be hyphenated once.
a wheel-barrow **b** ex-pla-na-tion
c sud-den-ly **d** re-mem-ber
e dic-tion-ary **f** quo-ta-tion

Dashes page 26
1 a I bought a beautiful ring — it looks good on my pig.
b When you are down, look up — people like to look at your face.
c She said — and she's always right — that dashes are often used incorrectly.
d My brother — the one with the long hair — plays in a rock band.
2 a I had a good day today — it was the weekend.
b The congregation said the prayer: You are mighty, O Lord — O Lord.
c 'The reason I was late — look at me.'
d Native trees — kauri, rimu, rātā, tītoki — will be planted in the forest

PART THREE: SENTENCES
pages 27-39

Run-on sentences page 27
1 a The rain had ceased at last. Leaves glistened as the wind played with them.
b I went to the beach. It was very windy and I lost my hat. Darn it!
c The riders revved their engines. The noise was deafening. The flag dropped and they were off.
d That is disgusting. (or '!') You wouldn't catch me eating any of the things they make them eat on *Survivor*. They must be desperate!
e It is essential that young people learn to eat properly. Childhood obesity is becoming a major problem world-wide. It must be stopped.
2 *Our suggestion:* The whole class waited. Ms Donovan had asked twice already and no one was leaving until the truth was out. So they waited. Not one person was brave enough to spill the beans, not even Megan. Their teacher stood at the front of the room, with her hands on her hips, staring at them. All of them.

Minor sentences page 28
The phrase
1 a during the holidays
b like a chook without its head
c A few hours later
d down the end of the tunnel
e after arriving late
2 a adverbial **b** adverbial **c** adjectival
d noun or adjectival **e** adjectival
3 Parent/guardian/teacher to check.
The subordinate clause
1 a after you have chosen one
b which has the most people in it
c which made everyone happy
d who came first in the Manu Kōrero speech contest
e Unless I study
2 a subordinate clause **b** phrase
c phrase **d** subordinate clause
e phrase

Simple sentences page 30
1 a Yes **b** No **c** Yes **d** Yes
e No **f** No **g** Yes

Compound sentences page 31
1 a Miles scored so/and the game was won.
b I want to hear the television so stop chewing.
c Rauhina had eggs for breakfast and/but Justin had toast.
d Jessica went to Otago and (or semicolon) Nile stayed in Dunedin but (or semi-colon) Josh went to Auckland.

e Minstrel was lame and Purdie was too old so Katie rode Willow.

f The weather had turned bad so the picnic was cancelled.

g Finished all my homework so time for computer games.

Complex sentences page 32

1 a my brother broke his finger
b I love my car
c Homework can help me understand my schoolwork
d Tom pushed him away
e The elderly woman brought the hankie to her mouth

2, 4, 5 Parent/guardian/teacher to check.

3 When Sophie brought her hand back into the light of the torch to check it, she was disgusted to see it covered in blood.
OR: Mrs Harvey was going nowhere in a huge hurry with that leg.

Compound-complex sentences page 34

1 It boomed out from the darkness, its source a bright square of light that turned out to be the Booths' garage yet people were outside, mainly huddled in little groups.

2, 3, 4 Parent/guardian/teacher to check.

Paragraphs pages 36-38

1 a 'Doctor, I get this dull flashing light in front of my eyes.'
'Try these,' the doctor said. 'That any better?'
'Much better. The flashing light is much brighter.'

b 'Why don't you ever listen to me?' wailed Melissa.
'What was that?' John asked.

c 'I hope there are some seats spare.'
'Me too,' she replied.
He turned to her. 'Haven't you got your ticket?'

d 'Where are you from, young man?'
'Small town south of Auckland,' was all Jeremy said.
'Me too,' trilled Megan.

e 'Here they come!'
'Who?' asked Trunk.
'Those repulsive, regurgitating creatures.'
'Wetas?' asked Naff.
'No,' replied Tizz. 'Teenagers!'

2 a She was fast ... far to go.
[Half an hour ... and unfriendly.

b She was completely ... began to cry.
[It had been about ... life.

c I trained for the ... to run.
[After six months ... competition.

d I went to buy ... late for work.
[A few minutes ... the counter.

e My monthly ... and I agreed.
[A week later, ... at the front.

3 a They played down ... were tired.
[Up at the house, ... trip home.

b Down at the dock, ... all day.
[At the warehouse, ... and excited.

c The waterfall ... stood mesmerised.
[Back at the ... fire started.

d Here we like ... any situation.
[In other countries ... like to think.

e On this side of ... a nervous parent.
[On the other side, ... the neighbourhood.

4 Zac looked about ... cigarette smoke.
[Against the wall, ... was saying.
[Putting the CD's ... the music.
[Mitch carried around ... the crowd.

Punctuation, grammar and sentence recap page 39

1 Brittany thought it was best she got it over with. 'I have something to say, Shannon: I am the one who told Toby that you liked him.'
Shannon's eyes widened and her cheeks flushed red. 'What? You did what?'
'I'm sorry. I thought I was helping. You see,' Brittany stammered, 'I overheard him on the bus talking to these two guys saying how much he liked you and did they know whether you liked him. The guys didn't know who you were and I — well — I thought that it wouldn't hurt to say, so I said!' Brittany's hands were sweaty; she felt a little dizzy with fear. Shannon was going to be so mad.
'How dare you! You cow! You — you — oh,' and Shannon began to cry.

2 Compare your work with a friend.

PART FOUR: WORD USE
pages 40-52

Prefixes pages 40-41

1 a super **b** anti **c** mis **d** epi
e under **f** re **g** hyper **h** non
i dis **j** ab
2 a ex **b** out **c** con **d** fore
e trans **f** pre **g** dis **h** uni
i post **j** pro
3 a tri (three) **b** ex (make bigger)
c anti (opposed to, against)
d de (down from, away)
e mis (wrongly, badly)
f dia (through, across, during)
4 Parent/guardian/teacher to check.

Suffixes pages 42-43

1 Parent/guardian/teacher to check.
2 a ly **b** ful **c** ment **d** ise
e able **f** ty/ity **g** ed **h** teen
i ist **j** wise
3 a cide **b** gram, graph
c crat, graph **d** logical
e culture **f** dom **g** icitis **h** hood
i culture/graph/gamy/gram
j cratic, logical, path
4 a ness **b** ence **c** tory **d** let
e ion **f** less
5 Parent/guardian/teacher to check.

Synonyms page 44

1 small_____tiny
over_____above
green_____emerald
tall_____lofty
call_____yell
porch_____veranda
chew_____gnaw
van_____minibus
shrub_____bush

2 a odour **b** circular **c** beautiful
d empty **e** yearly
3 Parent/guardian/teacher to check.

Antonyms page 45

1 entrance_____exit
arrive _____depart
shout _____whisper
married _____single
weak _____strong
happy_____sad
small_____big
dark_____light
starving_____full
private_____public

2 a discourage **b** background
c decrease **d** import
e misunderstand **f** disagree
g impossible **h** unload
i maximum **j** female
3 *Our suggestions:*
a tidy **b** failure **c** disobey
d apart **e** poor

Puns page 46

a Meaning one: *change* as in prices will come down.
Meaning two: *change* as in more money in your pocket.

b Meaning one: *bloody* as in covered in blood through injury.
Meaning two: *bloody* as in the swear word.

c Meaning one: *bun fight* as in a fight over hot cross buns.
Meaning two: *bun fight* as in a family argument.

d Meaning one: *Good Friday* as in the public holiday at Easter.
Meaning two: *Good Friday* as in a 'good' (great) day shopping.

e Meaning one: *stay on top* as in to float on the surface of the water.
Meaning two: *stay on top* as in maintaining control of the situation.

f Meaning one: *got a lot of cheek* as in she has a lot of bottom (a big bottom or lots of bottoms to put nappies on). Meaning two: *got a lot of cheek* as in she has a cheeky personality to be demanding a certain product.

Clichés page 47

1 a It's raining cats and dogs.
b Keeping up with the Joneses.
c Good as gold.
d Breath of fresh air.
e Crowning glory.
f Life and soul of the party.
g No stone left unturned.
h The coast is clear.
i Storm in a teacup.
j Hit the nail on the head.
k At the end of the day.

2 a good for nothing, skating on thin ice, draw the line, live in the lap of luxury, tarred with the same brush, putting my foot down
b heart of gold, long in the tooth, rules ... with an iron fist, sour grapes, rule the roost, plenty of get up and go, burnt the midnight oil, wet the baby's head

Colloquial language page 48

1 a Man, rip-off
b shoot through, hit the sack
c You beauty, spot on
d guys, muck around
e O.K.

2 a frustrated/angry (e.g. he's salty)
b agreeing with something
c cool
d gross
e to embarrass or insult someone
f be upset or offended by something
g go get MacDonalds
h mission; hard to do 'that was a mish and a half'
i that's bad or unappealing
j to impress someone in the hope that they will be romantically interested in you

Slang page 49

1 a ass **b** plonker
c butt **d** God
e twat

Jargon page 50

1 a Certificate of Title___lawyer
  b amps_____electrician
  c leeward_____sailor
  d pyroclastic flow_____vulcanologist
  e crampon_____mountain climber
  f haemoglobin_____doctor
  g carat_____jeweller
  h *Mentha spicata*_____biologist
  i URL_____computer user

2 a single lens reflex, shutter speed and aperture, zoom lens, EF system, USM and Image Stabiliser Lens, Advanced Integrated Multi-point control system, six-zone evaluative light metering
  b Accounts Receivable, General and Subsidiary ledgers, list of debtors, Current Liabilities, net and gross profits

Word use recap pages 51-52

1 Prefix: pre, re, to, bio, ex, inter, un, in, com, over, co, vice, poly, bi, fore
  Suffix: ment, able, ly, ist, ful, ing, er, ed, ise
2 fraud, odour, empty, rapidly, fatigued
3 a under b up c in d far
  e outside f after g in front h off
  i above j without
4 a fastest (superlative)
  b most food (superlative)
  c worst-dressed (superlative)
  d more tired (comparative)
  e luckier (comparative)
5 a Don't go overboard with booze.
  b up with the birds, may the force be with you
  c guys, yep, goin', tinnies, Bazza, avo, booze, sweet, mate, ta
  d bugger
  e knots, GPS, Fish-Finder

PART FIVE: MORE POETIC TECHNIQUES pages 53-56

Simile page 53

1 a He/death
    He looked terrible/pale/very sick/ lacking movement
  b Sky/black velvet
    The sky was very dark.
  c She/Lionel Messi
    She was an awesome soccer player
  d Cords/spider web
    There were many cords and they were all mixed/tied/mingled together.

Metaphor page 53

1 a Focus of thoughts changes/leaps around.
  b The politician has the same personality as a fox – sneaky/cunning/clever/ devious etc.
  c They had too many orders. A lot of orders were coming in.
  d If an apple cart is upset then the apples fall all over the place. The plans were now ruined.

Personification page 54

1 a A warm wind blew over the people sunbathing.
  b As the car went over the bumps the headlights were sometimes obscured so it looked like they were blinking.
  c The clouds were moving quickly across the sky.
  d A gap under the door allowed a cold wind to come into the house.

Alliteration page 55

1 a M: Milly/must/made/might/mess/mum
  b S: she/so/starving/she/seriously

c W: Winter/weather/wet/windy
d T: Tania/Tiktoker/tremendous
e K: koro/kind/kickboxing

Onomatopoeia page 55

1 a clanked b squelched c Argh
  d whizzed e whacked

Assonance page 56

1 a We needed to try to **light** the **fire**.
  b My Aunty was a huge **rock** and **roll** fan.
  c He gave a **nod** to the **officer** with the **pocket**.
  d You are going to **make** me **late**.
  e **Saving** the **whales** is a crucial **detail** to environmental groups.

Rhyme page 56

1 a he/see b circus/McGurkus
  c Enormance/performance
  d down/town
2 Parent/guardian/teacher to check.

PART SIX: IMPROVING YOUR CLOSE READING pages 42-60

Scanning page 57

1 8577 1435 2 6pm

Putting them all together page 58

b Coca (the dog).
c Under a lemon tree.
d Shout.
e Something about the way the shout sounded.

PART SEVEN: PRACTISING CLOSE READING pages 61-67

Passage one pages 61-62

1 A camp (in Culverden) *(1 mark)*
2 Any **two** of the following:
  Image: 'All the little townships sprinkled throughout the area' (metaphor)
  Explanation: The small towns were spread throughout the district; were everywhere in the area; were located randomly; were scattered/dotted; were not in an orderly fashion.
  Image: '... little townships sprinkled throughout the area sat *comfortably* ...' (personification)
  Explanation: the houses suited the countryside; looked like they belonged; were in the same style as the environment.
  Image: '... at the *foot* of the Southern Alps' (personification)
  Explanation: The houses were situated at the bottom/base of the mountains. *(4 marks)*
  Do not accept 'end' or 'beginning' of the Southern Alps. *(1 mark for image; 1 mark for explanation)*
  Note: *They do not get a mark for identifying the type of image. They do not need to identify the actual 'image' word, that is 'sprinkled' or 'foot', but they should start doing this.*
3 Because he was no longer in the city where it was busy and had a lot of people ... vast areas of natural environment ... not densely populated.
  Not: wide open space, free from clutter/ cluttered, populated North Island, quiet/ peaceful, pure and clear. *(1 mark)*
  Note: *Students need to be very aware that if the passage asks for 'in your own words' this is exactly what is meant.*
4 A rock formation. *(1 mark)*
5 A rise in the road. *(1 mark)*
6 It looked remarkably *like* a squatting frog. (paragraph 6) *(1 mark)*
  Note: *Students should again learn to underline the actual word or words that identify the feature.*

7 The atmosphere was slightly tense as night fell and made it more difficult to see. Jeremy was feeling increasingly uncomfortable or isolated. *(1 mark)*

Passage two pages 63-64

1 Because she dyed her hair (a different colour to her natural colour). *(1 mark)*
2 The senior girl. *(1 mark)*
3 Simile. *(1 mark)*
4 Because she wanted to look nicer/because it was what everyone else was doing/because it was popular. *(1 mark)*
5 'She completed her sentence/no bail allowed.' *(1 mark)*
6 The poet is comparing the senior student's punishment to someone going to prison for breaking the law. Her punishment (to cover books) is her 'sentence' and she must stay there for the whole time, not be let off earlier ('no bail allowed'). *(1 mark)*
7 Because she has also dyed her hair *(1 mark for reason)*. Not to be fashionable but to 'lie' about her age, to 'cheat time' (not look older) and to 'steal hope' by making herself look younger by colouring her hair. It helps her not to think about growing old. *(1 mark for evidence)*
8 She feels sorry for her because she only did something harmless and innocent. *(1 mark for reason.)* She thinks she 'should have sent her away ... laughing'. *(1 mark for evidence.)*

Passage three pages 65-66

1 Looking for objects on the beach that have been washed up (from ships) by the tide. *(1 mark)*
2 They are brothers 'My little brother ...' and/or '... I was first born'. *(1 mark for relationship.)* They sometimes fight 'my little brother can be tough'./Robbie likes to think he is braver than his older brother 'Don't be a sissy' and '... he was stronger and tougher than me.' *(1 mark for evidence.)*
3 He thinks that having a grown up with them will be helpful because their Grandad will know what to do. *(1 mark)*
4 Colloquial. *(1 mark)*
5 Alliteration. *(1 mark)*
6 Hissed. *(1 mark)*
7 Anything reasonable. Teacher to use professional judgement. *(1 mark)*
8 Charlie: cautious, uneasy, nervous
  Robbie: excited, curious, braver
  (2 marks, 1 mark for each boy, two responses required to gain full marks.)

Passage four pages 67-68

1 Because the wood is needed to make fence posts for a new fence by the creek. *(1 mark)*
2 To emphasise how sad/destructive it is. *(1 mark)*
3 That the rain doesn't want to see what is happening. That the rain is crying. That the rain is cutting itself off from seeing the lack of trees. *(1 mark)*
4 Any ONE of: Personification
              Metaphor
  (Repetition is also acceptable) *(1 mark)*
5 Because they have had the branches cut off them. There are no leaves/boughs left on them. *(1 mark)*
6 'Knobbly nuts' OR (part of) Where all day small winds sound,/And all day long the sun plays hide and seek with shadows.
7 The birds have nowhere to nest in the trees. *(2 marks)*
8 *Our suggestion:* She uses negative words like 'trodden' and 'stripped'. This suggests she thinks that it is a waste to destroy the trees. The poet talks about them being 'kind and friendly' trees. They can see the positive features of leaving nature as it is, for example: The noise of the branches waving in the wind and the use of the tree as homes for other animals. *(2 marks)*

2 **Use some, or all, of the following simple sentences, phrases and subordinate clauses, and add conjunctions to make a** compound-complex sentence.

My friend Fred.   Who loved to go to the movies.   I was surprised.
The film was exciting.   By a silly part.   He hoped to get seats.
With two tickets.

_____

_____

_____

_____

_____

_____

_____

3 **Write down your own** compound-complex sentence.

_____

_____

_____

_____

_____

4 **For the sentence you wrote in question 3, identify the parts:**

Simple sentences:

_____

_____

Phrases (if any) and/or subordinate clauses (if any):

_____

_____

_____

PARAGRAPHS

The purpose of the paragraph is to show a change of speaker during dialogue, to show other important changes or to group sentences that have something in common.

Without paragraphs, your writing is harder to read because it makes it more difficult to follow the ideas of the story or the stages of an argument.

Paragraphs are created in the following ways: either by indenting (starting the first line of the paragraph further in than the rest of the text) or by missing a line. Though there are no strict rules about when to use a new paragraph, here are some helpful guidelines.

A new paragraph when there is a change of topic

If you break up the ideas of your story or your essay, then the reader is more able to follow the line of your discussion. It also means that you need to organise your ideas so that you talk about one topic at a time.

If the paragraph is too long, then readers have to try to sort out your thoughts on their own and this can take away the enjoyment of reading what you have to say.

A new paragraph when there is a change of speaker

The best way to let your reader know who is talking, is to give each speaker a new paragraph when he or she speaks. That way, you don't have to always say, 'Charles said …', 'Mary replied …'.

For example, compare the following two extracts. In the first, it's quite difficult to work out who is speaking. The second is a lot clearer.

1   *'Did you have any of this before we left?'*
The man held up a piece of bread. 'Nope.
Why?' The man was silent for a time. 'Someone's
been in here.' 'Why do ya say that?'
'Dunno. Just get this feeling.
Check your stuff.'

2   *'Did you have any of this before we*
left?' The man held up a piece of bread.

'Nope. Why?'

The man was silent for a time. 'Someone's been in here.'

'Why do ya say that?'

'Dunno. Just get this feeling. Check your stuff.'

ISBN: 9780170462990   PHOTOCOPYING OF THIS PAGE IS RESTRICTED UNDER LAW.

1   **Using a red pen, put in the sign [to show where a new paragraph should be.**

a. 'Doctor, I get this dull flashing light in front of my eyes.' 'Try these,' the doctor said. 'That any better?' 'Much better. The flashing light is much brighter.'

b. 'Why don't you ever listen to me?' wailed Melissa. 'What was that?' John asked.

c. 'I hope there are some seats spare.' 'Me too,' she replied. He turned to her. 'Haven't you got your ticket?'

d. 'Where are you from, young man?' 'Small town south of Auckland,' was all Jeremy said. 'Me too,' trilled Megan.

e. 'Here they come!' 'Who?' asked Trunk. 'Those repulsive, regurgitating creatures.' 'Wetas?' asked Naff. 'No,' replied Tizz. 'Teenagers!'

A new paragraph when time has passed

When you want to show that the passing of time is important in a story, you should create a new paragraph. Your new paragraph might begin with such phrases as: *Later on that day ...; That night ...; An hour later ...; A year had passed when ...* and so on.

2   **Using a red pen, put in the sign [to show where a new paragraph should be.**

a. She was fast getting in a thoroughly bad mood. Thank goodness they hadn't far to go. Half an hour later they were travelling along a rarely used side road. It was windy and unfriendly.

b. She was completely lost. She couldn't see any roads and the gentle breeze brought no sounds of humanity. With tears welling up in her eyes, Sophie began to cry. It had been about sixteen hours since the accident and now Sophie began to seriously fear for Mrs Harvey's life.

c. I trained for the marathon every day, getting up at five in the mornings to run. After six months, I felt I was ready and entered my first serious competition.

d. I went to buy some movie tickets but the cinema centre hadn't opened yet. A man was standing outside the doors and I spent some time complaining to him how it was poor service to be kept waiting. He agreed and then excused himself as he was late for work. A few minutes later, the doors opened and when I went to buy my ticket, the man I had been speaking to was behind the counter.

e. My monthly meeting with the principal went smoothly until I mentioned that my students were considering protesting about the poor standard of food in the canteen. He suggested I set an example by eating the food on the menu and I agreed. A week later, the principal opened his office door to the sound of students protesting — with me at the front.

A new paragraph when there is a change of place

Characters in a story can move from room to room, house to house, city to city or country to country. If their move is important, then you should give it a new paragraph. For example:

Zac lay awake wondering what would have happened to him if he had not met Molly. Perhaps his life would've been simpler; less exciting, sure, but at least predictable. He felt exhausted trying to work it all out so he got out of bed to get a drink of water.

In the kitchen, the glow from the moon lit up everything and he quenched his thirst without needing to turn on the light.

 Using a red pen, put in the sign [to show where a new paragraph should be.

a. They played down by the river most of the afternoon. It had been fun and they were tired. Up at the house, preparations were being made for the long trip home.

b. Down at the dock, the men unloaded the cargo. It took all day. At the warehouse, Jimmy waited for them to come. He was nervous and excited.

c. The waterfall dropped eight metres and was stunning in its power and beauty. They had tramped all day to see it and now stood mesmerised. Back at the campsite, Tasha set up the tent and got the fire started.

d. Here we like to think that we are unique; that we have initiative and can make the most of any situation. In other countries where people have lived for many hundreds of years, they rely on tradition and systems to help them through — well, that's what we like to think.

e. On this side of the river, Manly grazed expensive deer. He had paid fourteen hundred dollars a head and watched over them like a nervous parent. On the other side, Brad kept his aging sheep; the ones he hadn't the heart to send to the meat works. And always, Manly wondered what he could do to improve the neighbourhood.

A new paragraph when there is a change of person

When someone new comes into a story, it is a good idea to 'introduce' them by starting a new paragraph. If someone has already been 'introduced' but they go out of the storyline and then come back, and it is important, then the same principle applies. For example:

Mr Montgomery sat at his desk staring at the books before him. He had promised his class that they would be marked by today but it was unlikely he would be able to get them done.

Jonathan Wilkes stared at the test paper: he had promised his parents that this time he would not fail but, judging by the questions and his lack of study, it was unlikely he would pass.

 Using a red pen, put in the sign [to show where a new paragraph should be.

Zac looked about the room. It was filled with people from the hostel as well as the thick haze of cigarette smoke. Against the wall, Louise stood talking intently with the guy from his Statistics course. She was shorter than him and he had to keep leaning forward to hear what she was saying. Putting the CD's in order was Allan, the original party animal. He knew as much as anybody about what was hot and what was not and so Zac agreed to let him control the music. Mitch carried around the trays of food though most of it was being consumed by the members of the first fifteen. She was tall and moved easily through the crowd.

ISBN: 9780170462990   PHOTOCOPYING OF THIS PAGE IS RESTRICTED UNDER LAW.

PUNCTUATION, GRAMMAR AND SENTENCE RECAP

1 You be the proof reader. The following passage has many punctuation errors. Using a red pen put in the missing dashes, exclamation marks, question marks, colons, semi-colons and paragraphs. You may like to mark it in pencil first.

Brittany thought it was best she got it over with. 'I have something to say, Shannon. I am the one who told Toby that you liked him.' Shannon's eyes widened and her cheeks flushed red. 'What. You did what.' 'I'm sorry. I thought I was helping. You see,' Brittany stammered, 'I overheard him on the bus talking to these two guys saying how much he liked you and did they know whether you liked him. The guys didn't know who you were and I well I thought that it wouldn't hurt to say so I said.' Brittany's hands were sweaty she felt a little dizzy with fear. Shannon was going to be so mad. 'How dare you. You cow. You you oh,' and Shannon began to cry.

2 Beside each of the following terms, write down how many you wrote for the **above** extract:

exclamation marks _____   question marks _____

colons _____   semi-colons _____

dashes _____   minor sentences _____

complex sentences _____   compound-complex sentences _____

paragraphs _____

ISBN: 9780170462990

PREFIXES

A prefix is a group of letters added to the beginning of a word to change its meaning or form a new word.

Prefixes are letters or short words placed before other words. To understand them you need to know a little about the history of the English language. Many prefixes come from Latin or Greek words and have been incorporated into English. Once you understand the meaning of a prefix you can see how many words have been formed.

Let's take a look at two common prefixes:

sub Sub means under — what words can you think of that include sub? What about sub*marine* (underwater boat) or sub*way* (underground railway)? Can you think of any more? Sub*merge*, sub*mit*, sub*ordinating*, sub*normal* all have to do with being beneath or under someone/something.

re Re means back or again. Look at the words re*join*, re*turn* or re*count*, re*peat* or re*prise* … they all have a common thread, that of doing something again.

1 **Underline the prefixes in the following words.**

a. superman
b. anticlockwise
c. mislead
d. epidural
e. underneath
f. reassess
g. hypermarket
h. nonsmoker
i. disappear
j. absent

2 **Choose a prefix from the box to complete the words below.**

out	trans	pro	ex	fore
pre	post	uni	dis	con

a. _____ hale
b. _____ sider
c. _____ clusion
d. _____ see
e. _____ port
f. _____ cook
g. _____ count
h. _____ corn
i. _____ pone
j. _____ ject

ISBN: 9780170462990

3 Each list can be completed by the same prefix. Put an appropriate prefix and then explain its meaning.

a. _____ pod

_____ angle

_____ plets

_____ cycle

Meaning _____

b. _____ pand

_____ tend

_____ aggerate

_____ port

Meaning _____

c. _____ septic

_____ social

_____ dote

_____ perspirant

Meaning _____

d. _____ scend

_____ part

_____ crease

_____ struct

Meaning _____

e. _____ take

_____ lead

_____ spell

_____ behave

Meaning _____

f. _____ logue

_____ gonal

_____ meter

_____ gram

Meaning _____

4 Now create your own lists of prefixes. Perhaps you could test your peers (or parents) and see if they can complete your exercise. You may like to use a dictionary to help you come up with the words.

For example: *Phillip chose the prefix 'under' and gave it to Dave to complete. He came up with: underpants, undergraduate, underworld, undersourced.*

a. _____

_____

_____

_____

Meaning _____

b. _____

_____

_____

_____

Meaning _____

c. _____

_____

_____

_____

Meaning _____

d. _____

_____

_____

_____

Meaning _____

ISBN: 9780170462990

SUFFIXES

A suffix is one or more letters added to the end of a word to alter its meaning.

You will be familiar with some of the most common suffixes used in English: -ing, -ed and -s, but there are many others.

1 **List five other** common suffixes **that you use in your work. Remember to only list the suffix — not the whole word.**

a. _____

b. _____

c. _____

d. _____

e. _____

Compare these with other members of your class (or whoever is at home) and add five more that you didn't think of.

f. _____

g. _____

h. _____

i. _____

j. _____

2 **Using a red pen, underline the** suffix **in the following words.**

a. confidently

b. beautiful

c. investment

d. criticise

e. tolerable

f. equality

g. fidgeted

h. sixteen

i. chemist

j. clockwise

ISBN: 9780170462990

3 Choose a suffix from the box below to complete the words. Be careful. There are more in the box than you need.

culture	logical	crat	dom	genic
gon	ism	gamy	mantic	meter
cide	cratic	path	icitis	
hood	graph	gram	ferous	

a. fungi _____   b. picto _____

c. demo _____   d. chrono _____

e. viti _____   f. king _____

g. append _____   h. false _____

i. mono _____   j. socio _____

4 Look carefully at the following words and choose the suffix that completes them all.

a. bright _____   b. exist _____   c. observa _____

   kind _____   pati _____   dormi _____

   dark _____   depend _____   fac _____

d. book _____   e. creat _____   f. point _____

   pig _____   situat _____   hope _____

   leaf _____   inject _____   care _____

5 Now create your own lists of suffixes like those in question 4. Perhaps you could test your peers (or parents) and see if they can complete your exercise. You may like to use a dictionary to help you come up with the words.

For example: *Sio chose the suffix 'late' and gave it to Emma to complete. She came up with: articulate, translate, postulate, hyperventilate.*

a. _____ _____   b. _____ _____

   _____ _____   _____ _____

   _____ _____   _____ _____

   _____ _____   _____ _____

c. _____ _____   d. _____ _____

   _____ _____   _____ _____

   _____ _____   _____ _____

ISBN: 9780170462990

SYNONYMS

Synonyms are words that have the same meanings as other words.

A thesaurus is full of synonyms, as its job is to tell us other words we could use. Using synonyms helps to improve our writing and vocabulary. It is a good idea to change at least two words in each piece of writing you do in order to liven up your writing and extend your vocabulary.

1 **Link the words in the left-hand column with their** synonyms.

small	minibus
over	yell
green	bush
tall	emerald
call	veranda
porch	lofty
chew	above
van	tiny
shrub	gnaw

2 **Replace the word in brackets with its** synonym **from the box.**

empty	strong	mini	odour	penthouse
square	yearly	circular	beautiful	big

a. The (smell) _____ of the room made my stomach churn.

b. The (round) _____ container did not fit easily into the chillybin.

c. Catherine was the most (pretty) _____ little girl I had met.

d. The (vacant) _____ apartment next to mine had finally been rented.

e. The (annual) _____ fishing competition was on this weekend.

3 **In the space provided, write a** synonym **for the given word.**

a. beautiful _____   **b.** kind _____

c. thin _____   **d.** film _____

e. rubbish _____   **f.** cry _____

g. considered _____   **h.** asked _____

ISBN: 9780170462990

ANTONYMS

An antonym is a word that is opposite in meaning to the given word.

As the prefix 'anti' suggests, an antonym is a word that is the opposite of a chosen word. For example, the opposite of big is small, therefore *small* is an antonym of *big*.

Antonyms can be formed by:
a.	a new word	*e.g.*	*fail*	*pass*
b.	adding a prefix	*e.g.*	*natural*	*unnatural*
c.	changing a prefix	*e.g.*	*interior*	*exterior*
d.	changing a suffix	*e.g.*	*employee*	*employer*

1 **Link the antonyms in the following lists by drawing a line between them.**

entrance	full
arrive	big
shout	exit
married	light
weak	depart
happy	single
small	whisper
dark	strong
starving	public
private	sad

2 **Create antonyms for the given words by either changing or adding a prefix.**

a. encourage _____   **b.** foreground _____

c. increase _____   **d.** export _____

e. understand _____   **f.** agree _____

g. possible _____   **h.** load _____

i. minimum _____   **j.** male _____

3 **To change the meaning of the sentence, replace the words in brackets with its antonym.**

a. My daughter is wonderful at making her bed. It always looks (messy) _____.

b. My revision programme for the exams had been a brilliant (success) _____.

c. I had decided it might be best to (obey) _____ my parents' curfew tonight.

d. Family reunions are an interesting phenomenon — we're much better (together) ___.

e. Isn't it wonderful to be (rich) _____?

PUNS

A pun is an expression that plays on different meanings of the same word or phrase.

To create a pun, there needs to be a word that is identical (or similar) in sound but can be used in different ways. Although puns are more often used for humorous purposes, they can also have a serious effect.

For example, a poster warning of the dangers of drinking and boating might read:
Don't go overboard with booze this summer. The two meanings are: don't fall out of the boat (go overboard) and don't drink too much (go overboard on the alcohol).

1 **Read the following advertising slogans carefully. Using a red pen, underline the pun and in the space provided write the two meanings of the word.**

a. A large retail store advertised: **'This winter you can expect change from our prices'**.

Meaning one: _____

Meaning two: _____

b. A drink-driving advertisement: **'If you drink and drive, you're a bloody idiot'**.

Meaning one: _____

Meaning two: _____

c. An advertisement for hot cross buns read: **'Buy plenty. Don't have a bun fight this Easter!'**.

Meaning one: _____

_____

Meaning two: _____

d. A company used: **'Make sure you have a Good Friday by shopping with us'** on their Easter weekend flyer.

Meaning one: _____

Meaning two: _____

e. An advertisement for water safety: **'Use a life jacket and stay on top'**.

Meaning one: _____

Meaning two: _____

f. A Huggies nappy advert read: **'She likes Huggies so much she demands them. Boy, she's got a lot of cheek'**.

Meaning one: _____

Meaning two: _____

ISBN: 9780170462990

CLICHÉS

A cliché is a trite, dull expression that has lost its originality and humour through constant use.

Clichés are familiar phrases that you hear in everyday speech. Once they were hip and modern but due to them being over-used, they have lost their freshness.

You should try to avoid using clichés in your own writing because they can give the impression that you haven't given much thought to your work.

1 **Link the clichés in the columns below.**

It's raining	clear.
Keeping up	left unturned.
Good	a teacup.
Breath of	of the day.
Crowning	on the head.
Life and soul	with the Joneses.
No stone	cats and dogs.
The coast is	as gold.
Storm in	fresh air.
Hit the nail	of the party.
At the end	glory.

2 **Using a red pen, underline the clichés in the following passages.**

a. You good for nothing dog! Those were my best slippers. You are skating on thin ice now, my boy. I absolutely draw the line at shoe chewing. You live in the lap of luxury and still you can't behave yourself. How many other dogs do you know that get sirloin steak every night? You and that cat are tarred with the same brush. Well, I'm putting my foot down as of now — there will be no more sleeping in my bed.

b. My nana has a heart of gold — she may be a little long in the tooth but she rules our family with an iron fist. Sometimes Mum suffers from sour grapes. Secretly I think she would like to rule the roost. Nana has plenty of get up and go. When her first grandchild was born, she burnt the midnight oil with the rest of us. Boy, did we wet the baby's head!

STYLES OF LANGUAGE

Before we start this section, you need to be aware of the different types of language styles used in English. In most cases this is referred to as *register*. Register is a style of language characteristics that belong to a particular social situation. It is important that you have a basic knowledge of the different styles of language, and of the appropriate places to use them, so that you can create the correct tone for your piece of writing or character.

Slang	Colloquial	Formal	Frozen Formal
	Common conversation Personal letters and diaries	News articles Non-fiction books Essays	Legal contracts

Colloquial language
Colloquial language is relaxed and informal language that is used in common conversation.

Colloquial language is everyday conversation language used among friends and family. New Zealand has a wide range of colloquial terms that are sometimes shared with Australia. Colloquial expressions are no less important than formal English but as with all writing, you need to use it appropriately. It is most likely you will use colloquial language in your creative writing in order to give it some originality and make it sound real. You may also study colloquial language on its own in the senior school.

 1 **Choose the appropriate** colloquial phrase **or** word **from the box to complete the sentences below.**

Man	hit the sack	You beauty
shoot through	spot on	guys
muck around	O.K.	rip-off

a. _____ , look at the price of those jeans. What a _____ .

b. I'm gonna _____ . I want to _____ early tonight.

c. _____ , you hit the wicket _____ .

d. Come on, _____ . We'll miss the start if you _____ much longer.

e. _____ , let's get down to business.

ISBN: 9780170462990

2 **Write the actual meaning of the following** colloquial phrases **in the space provided.**

a. salty _____

b. chur _____

c. sick _____

d. rank _____

e. roast _____

f. cut up _____

g. maccas run _____

h. mish _____

i. rats _____

j. slay _____

Slang

Slang is the term given to words or expressions that belong to a particular group of people, and is, in most cases, considered unacceptable language.

Slang also joins colloquial language at the end of the continuum. Although both slang and colloquial expressions are very similar in style, slang is even more relaxed. The expression 'slang' comes from the historical language of thieves and disreputable people, and today slang is still considered inappropriate in most situations as it is often rude and offensive.

Another distinction of slang expressions is that they usually belong to a particular group of people and are therefore not as widely understood as colloquial ones. They tend to change very quickly as they are associated with 'in' fads and fashions. You should only use slang in your English work if it is appropriate to both the character and the situation.

1 **Read the following sentences carefully. Using a red pen, underline the** slang word/s **in the sentence and then rewrite the sentences using appropriate language.**

a. 'Shut your face, you ass.'

_____

b. All I said to the principal was 'he was a plonker' and now I'm in Saturday detention.

_____

c. Bart Simpson's voice rang out loud and clear: 'Kiss my butt.'

_____

d. God, I hate my Science teacher.

_____

e. You're behaving like such a twat.

_____

Jargon
Jargon is specialised language used by people who work together or share a common interest.

Jargon is a special type of language that is developed by a group of people who are dealing with the same topic. Almost every interest, occupation or sport has a terminology that is understood only by its members or employees. For example, surfers and skateboarders have their own language, as do doctors and lawyers.

The advantage of using jargon is that it helps people communicate quickly and effectively with each other as they do not have to use longwinded explanations and definitions. However, it does make it difficult for newcomers as, until they get up to speed with the vocabulary involved, they could be at a bit of a loss.

1 **Match the jargon in the left column with the appropriate occupation in the right.**

Certificate of Title	jeweller
amps	biologist
leeward	doctor
pyroclastic flow	mountain climber
crampon	sailor
haemoglobin	lawyer
carat	electrician
Mentha spicata	vulcanologist
URL	computer user

2 **Using your red pen, underline the jargon in the following passages.**

a. It is everything you expect from a single lens reflex camera and more. Explore creative photography by manually selecting the shutter speed and aperture. It uses built-in intelligence with the standard zoom lens (or choose from over 50 other lenses from the EF system). Sample the technology of a USM and Image Stabiliser Lens, along with the Advanced Integrated Multi-point control system. The latter allows six-zone evaluative light metering while still being compact and affordable.

b. There is a lot to achieve today, team. The Accounts Receivable column does not balance and we still have the General and Subsidiary ledgers to review. Have you finished the list of debtors, Michelle? And could you please calculate the Current Liabilities and then add them with your report on the net and gross profits, Sarah? Right, we need to make a dent in this by two o'clock. We'll touch base again then.

ISBN: 9780170462990

WORD USE RECAP

Let's put into practice what you have learnt. Before you complete the activities, carefully read the definitions of the items covered in this section to remind yourself of their meanings and uses.

- A **prefix** is a group of letters added to the beginning of a word to change its meaning or form a new word.

- A **suffix** is a group of letters added to the end of a word to alter its meaning.

- A **synonym** is a word that has the same meaning as another word.

- An **antonym** is a word that is opposite in meaning to the given word.

- **Colloquial language** is relaxed and informal language that is used in common conversation.

- A **cliché** is a trite, dull expression that has lost its originality and humour through constant use.

- **Slang** is words or expressions that belong to a particular group of people, for instance a class or set. In most cases they are not considered acceptable language.

- **Jargon** is specialised language used by people who work together or share a common interest.

1 **Read the following lists carefully. Using a red pen, circle the** prefixes **and underline the** suffixes**.**

ment	re	ly	ful	ing	com	ed	poly
pre	to	ist	inter	er	over	vice	bi
able	bio	ex	un	in	co	ise	fore

2 **Using a red pen, circle the word in Column B that is** nearest in meaning **to the given word in Column A.**

Column A	Column B		
fake	family	faulty	fraud
smell	tone	odour	fumes
vacant	empty	gone	alone
quickly	rapidly	cleverly	pace
tired	energetic	fatigued	quiet

3 Give the appropriate antonym for the following prepositions.

a. over _____

b. down _____

c. out _____

d. near _____

e. inside _____

f. before _____

g. behind _____

h. on _____

i. below _____

j. with _____

4 Each sentence below contains either a comparative or a superlative. Identify which it is by underlining the word/s and write comparative or superlative in the space provided.

a. I was the fastest runner in my class. _____

b. I ate the most food at the party. _____

c. The prize went to the worst-dressed person. _____

d. She was more tired than me so I let her rest. _____

e. Uncle Tim is always luckier than Dad. _____

5 Read the following passage carefully. Then, in the spaces below, write as many examples of each of the identified items as you can find.

'You guys are up with the birds. Off for a fish?'
'Yep, we're trying to catch the tide.'
'How long you goin' for?'
'Back later tonight. Bit of a bugger about the party being put off. At least it saves us buying more tinnies to take with us.'
'What's the forecast?'
'Fifteen knots from the nor'-east, slight swell.'
'Got your GPS and Fish-Finder installed?'
'Yep, Bazza did it yesterday avo.'
'Well, may the force be with you and remember, "don't go overboard with booze".'
'Yep, sweet mate, ta.'

a. Pun _____

b. Cliché _____

c. Colloquial _____

d. Slang _____

e. Jargon _____

ISBN: 9780170462990

IMAGERY

Imagery is a term used to cover a range of language techniques that all form mental images of things or events. They are lively descriptions that help us to paint a picture or create a movie in our heads.

Similes, metaphors and personification are all examples of imagery. A writer uses imagery in order to link two ideas and to create a vivid or life-like image in their audience's mind. Although you will no doubt be familiar with each of these techniques, let's take a moment to go over them once again.

Simile

A simile is a phrase that compares two things using 'like' or 'as'.

The best way to find a simile in a text is to ask yourself whether or not two unlike things are being compared. You will need to be able to:

- recognise a simile
- state what is being compared
- explain the literal meaning of the simile.

For example: *The students behaved like a pack of wild animals.*

Here the author has compared the students to a pack of wild animals. The literal meaning of this simile is that the students behaved like untamed animals. They were unruly, noisy and out of control.

1 **For each of the following sentences underline the two things being compared and then explain the meaning of the simile in the space provided.**

a. He looked like death when they found him.

This sentence means: _____

b. The sky looked like black velvet.

This sentence means: _____

c. She played soccer like she was Lionel Messi.

This sentence means: _____

d. The cords coming out of the back of the TV looked like a spider web.

This sentence means: _____

Metaphor

A metaphor is where one thing is said to be another.

Metaphors are like similes in that two things are compared, however they are different in that they do not use 'like' or 'as' but rather say that the two things are the same or equal.

For example: *The school students were a pack of wild animals.*

In this example, the school students are given the attributes of a 'pack of wild animals'. The literal attributes that are being given to the students are that they are noisy and out of control.

Explain the meaning of the following metaphors **in the space provided.**

a. Sometimes my train of thought gets off track.

This sentence means: _____

_____

b. The politician was a sly fox.

This sentence means: _____

_____

c. They were swamped with orders.

This sentence means: _____

_____

d. He upset the apple cart of their plans.

This sentence means: _____

Personification

When a non-living thing is given living characteristics or when a non-human thing is given human characteristics, it is called personification. Personification is a specific type of metaphor.

For example: *The old tree is an aged and tired man.*
Its knobbly fingers tremble, reaching out
For its withering brown hat, blown off in the wind.

In the first line of the above example the writer has stated that two objects, a tree and a man, are the same thing. The next two lines give the tree human characteristics. The trees limbs are 'knobbly fingers' and the tree has a 'brown hat' instead of leaves.

 For each of the following sentences underline the two things being compared and then explain the meaning of the personification in the space provided.

a. The sun's warm breath wafted over the sunbathers.

This sentence means: _____

b. The car's eyes blinked as it crossed the rough terrain.

This sentence means: _____

c. The clouds danced across the sky heralding the bad weather to come.

This sentence means: _____

_____

d. The cold draught snuck under the front door and crept up the stairs to chill the house.

This sentence means: _____

_____

SOUND EFFECTS

We have just spent some time reminding you how writers paint a picture for us by using words. The next set of techniques is used by writers to put a soundtrack to their picture. Simile, metaphor and personification help us to see what is happening, while alliteration, onomatopoeia, assonance and rhyme help us to hear what is happening which creates a particular atmosphere or mood.

Alliteration

Alliteration is the repetition of consonant sounds, usually at the beginning of words, in a sequence or phrase.

Alliteration occurs when there is a sequence of words that begin with, or have in them, the same letter sound. There are several reasons why alliteration is used. Firstly, it helps draw our attention to a line of a poem or a particular image the writer thought was important. Another reason is that it can slow down or speed up words to create an atmosphere.

 Underline the alliteration in the following sentences.

a. Milly must have made a mighty mess for her mum to be so mad.

b. Ali decided that she was so starving that she would seriously consider eating a horse.

c. Brrrrrr. Winter weather is wet and windy.

d. Tania was the best Tiktoker. She had a tremendous following.

e. My koro is kind unless if we interrupt him watching the kickboxing.

Onomatopoeia

Onomatopoeia is the formation of a word whose sound imitates or suggests the meaning or noise the action describes.

These 'sound words' are used to echo the action they make. They are used to help the reader experience what is happening by recalling the sound that something makes and thereby improving our ability to understand what is going on.

 Underline the onomatopoeia in each of the following sentences.

a. The saucepans clanked as they were packed into the dishwasher.

b. The flowing soap slowly squelched all over the bench as my three-year-old sister held down the pump.

c. Argh! Spider!

d. The fly whizzed around the room looking for an escape hatch.

e. James whacked the cricket ball.

ISBN: 9780170462990

Assonance
Assonance is the deliberate repetition of the same vowel sound followed by a different consonant sound.

Assonance is a difficult technique to identify. When we try to find assonance we are looking at the repetition of vowel sounds (and the following consonant sound/s) in the middle of words.

For example: *A stitch in time saves nine.*

See how the words 'time' and 'nine' both have the vowel 'i' as their dominant sound? For this to be recognised as assonance, they must have different consonants – one has **m** while the other one has **n**.

 Underline the assonance in the following sentences.

    a. We needed to try to light the fire.

    b. My aunty was a huge rock and roll fan.

    c. He gave a nod to the officer with the pocket.

    d. You are going to make me late.

    e. Saving the whales is a crucial detail to environmental groups.

Rhyme
Rhyme is the repetition of similar sounds, usually at the ends of lines.

Rhyme is usually used in order to be pleasing to the ear and to give a piece of writing rhythm and flow. It can also be used to link lines of poetry together in order to link ideas and images.

 Link the words that rhyme in each of the following excerpts of Dr Seuss books by joining them together with a line.

And today the Great Yertle, that Marvelous he
Is King of the Mud. That is all he can see.

All ready to put up the tents for my circus.
I think I will call it the Circus McGurkus.

And NOW comes an act of Enormous Enormance!
No former performer's performed this performance!

Go make the Oobleck tumble down
On every street, in every town.

 Use the internet to investigate the different types of rhyme used by writers. Write, on a separate piece of paper, a definition and example for each type you find.

ISBN: 9780170462990

IMPROVING YOUR CLOSE READING

Authors use the tools of language and grammar to manipulate how we feel, what images go into our head, and what we think about a particular topic. Each word has its own job in the sentence and when you can see why the author has chosen that particular word (or words) in that order, you are **comprehending** (understanding) the passage.

By now you should have a good knowledge of the basic language features of English, and more importantly, why they are used. It is time to take a look at how your understanding of these features will be tested. In most cases, it will be in an examination or test situation and will be referred to as 'close reading'. You will be asked to read a passage and complete the questions that follow. It is likely that you will be given a variety of extracts to read. Usually, the questions require you to identify what the author is saying (idea), how the author says it (technique) or why the author says it (purpose).

This section of the book focuses on how you can develop your close reading skills. First we will look at scanning and skimming, which are valuable for quickly identifying pieces of information in a text. Then we will concentrate on identifying the type of questions commonly used to test close reading and teach you the way to approach answering such questions. The third part of this section gives you a variety of practice passages.

Scanning and skimming

Not all reading is the same: sometimes you might be reading a story for enjoyment, another time searching for a particular word or number in a list *(scanning)*, or perhaps you might be browsing through a newspaper or magazine article looking for a specific fact *(skimming)*. When it comes to the study of English, scanning and skimming are useful skills to use when answering close reading questions. Being able to identify a key word or technique quickly will help you improve the efficiency of your answers. Let's take a quick look at each before we combine them to analyse a piece of text.

Scanning

Scanning is the quickest way to get information from a text. Instead of reading every word, your eyes are searching quickly through something looking for a specific thing. Some people use their finger or a ruler to help them scan down a list. In everyday life, scanning is used when you want to find a word in the dictionary or someone's phone number from a contact list.

 What is the phone number of Farteze Fine Foods? Underline the correct answer.

Farr Denis and Olive	8673 6547	Farrow K & L	8734 9987
Farrant Peter	3098 3323	Farteze Fine Foods	8577 1435
Farrell Dr B	8893 0093	Farvid David	5587 8823
Farrington Mr and Mrs T	3345 9245	Fasher Jane & Steven	4403 0093

 What time does the concert start? Underline the correct answer.

Parents and friends of all students are invited to attend the annual fundraising concert this Friday at 6pm in the school hall. Please fill out the form below to reserve your seat and send back with your child to school.

Skimming

Skimming is most commonly used to 'skim read' a written text to locate relevant information. It saves you time as you do not have to read (or in the case of close reading, **reread!**) the whole passage. Here are some general guidelines for skimming:

- **Identify the key words** (scanning) in the questions, which will show you where the answers are in the text;

- **Skim read the text** by sliding your eyes down the middle of the page or moving your finger across the page looking for key words;

- When you find **the key word, quickly read around** it to find the answer to the question.

Putting them all together

Below is a simple close reading exercise that will give you a chance to practise your scanning and skimming. Start by carefully reading the passage through (so you understand the piece as a whole) and answer the questions using the guidelines. We have helped you with question **a**.

Carl walked along the length of the fence until he found a gap to get through and squeezed in with Coca following. The frisbee was under a lemon tree. He didn't want to play any more. He wished his father would go on his ride now and not remind him about how annoying he was to his mum.

But, just as Carl bent down to pick it up, he heard his father shout and Coca growled. There was another shout and Coca barked again, tearing off through the fence. There was something in the way it sounded that made Carl's stomach chill.

Extract from *Space Gum* by Tania Roxborogh.

a. How did Carl get through the fence?

Identify the key word in the question: *fence*
Scan for the word fence in the passage: line 1
Skim read the sentence/s around it: ' ... *the length of the fence until he found a gap to get through and squeezed in ...* '
Write the answer to the question:

Carl found a gap in the fence and squeezed through it.

Now use the same technique to answer questions **b–e**. To help you we have highlighted the key words from each question in bold type.

b. Who **followed** him?

c. Where was the **frisbee**?

d. What did Carl **hear** his **father** do?

ISBN: 9780170462990   PHOTOCOPYING OF THIS PAGE IS RESTRICTED UNDER LAW.

e. What made Carl's **stomach chill**?

Recognising what the question is asking

Another skill that can help improve your close reading is understanding what the question is actually asking you. In other words, once you learn to recognise the 'type' of question you can give the marker the 'correct' response.

The types of questions asked can be categorised into three basic levels:

Level one: What do the words say?
Level two: What do the words mean?
Level three: Why did the author write this?

Let's take a careful look at each of these levels so you can begin to recognise what the question is actually asking you. Then you can give an appropriate answer.

Level one

The first level of question (Level one) is aimed to check that you understand what you have read. These questions deal with the **content** of the passage and ask you to reuse the information that is already used in the passage. For example:

1   **Culverden was 'on the way' to where?**

Or:

2   **What was Megan and Jeremy's destination?**

Level two

The next level of question (Level two) is where the English Basics books will help you the most. The questions may ask you to identify language features and they may go further and ask you to offer an explanation as to their meaning. For example:

1   **Write down an example of a simile from the passage.**

Or:

2   **What does 'crest' on line 19 mean?**

Level three

The final group of questions (Level three) relates to the style of the passages and may ask you to comment on the tone or type of language, the point-of-view of the passage or even why the passage was written (the purpose). For example:

1   **Describe the atmosphere of the final paragraph.**

Or:

2   **What is the writer's purpose?**

Being aware of what the question is asking you is an important skill you can learn when it comes to answering close reading questions. Before you move on to complete the following close reading activities, we suggest you quickly reread your *More English Basics* book, or at the least the glossary at the end of this book, to remind you of the language features you have studied. We have also given you some guidelines on how to tackle the various types of questions asked.

Guidelines to answering close reading questions

- Reread the question carefully. Ensure you understand exactly what is being asked of you. If they have not already been highlighted, underline key words.

- Go back to the passage and reread the area which you think mentions the answer. In some cases you will be given a reference point, either a line number or paragraph number. Always ensure you read around the area and keep in mind that any answer you give needs to relate to the passage. We call this 'keeping in context' with the passage.

- Watch for the following things:

  - 'In your own words …' – this means you cannot copy straight from the text but need to put the answer in your own words.

  - 'Give the word …' – if the question asks for a specific number of words make sure that is all you give.

  - 'Quote part of the sentence …' – quoting means you need to copy the exact words from the passage. If they only ask for part of a sentence, only choose the part that answers the question. Writing the whole sentence will make you lose marks.

  - 'In full sentences …' – if you are asked to give your answer in full sentences you will not be able to use note form.

- If you are unsure of what answer to put down, incorporate all the information you have. That way you have covered all the bases.

- Always make sure you give a full answer – you may only get half marks if you give a quick option.

- If you have been asked to identify a poetic technique or a particular word, you should get used to underlining the specific words in the sentence you copy. This shows that you actually know the technique and have not just taken a guess.

ISBN: 9780170462990   PHOTOCOPYING OF THIS PAGE IS RESTRICTED UNDER LAW.

PRACTISING CLOSE READING

Passage one

Read the following extract carefully and answer the questions that follow.

> Culverden was reached from inland North Canterbury and was on the way for travellers going to the West Coast via the Lewis Pass.
>
> All the little townships sprinkled throughout the area sat comfortably at the foot of the Southern Alps and enjoyed the extremes of South Island weather: high, dry temperatures in
> 5   the summer; deep snows in the winter. The air was pure and clear and the vast countryside quiet and peaceful.
>
> It all looked great to Jeremy. The wide open space that ran on towards the mountains was free from the clutter of the populated North Island. He felt sure he would have room to grow in this place.
> 10   The road began to curve and dip and was a strange contrast to the mainly long straight roads they had been travelling down for the last couple of hours.
>
> 'That's Frog Rock,' Paul said, pointing up to the formation that rose ahead of them. 'It's better if you look on the other side.'
>
> Megan and Jeremy twisted their necks to look back at the dusty orange cliff. It looked
> 15   remarkably like a squatting frog.
>
> 'And that's The Elephants over there,' Paul added, pointing across the valley to another series of cliffs. They were more obscure but Jeremy could just make out the outline of some elephant heads.
>
> They came over a crest and descended into Waikari, a small township that, on the welcome
> 20   board, boasted ancient Māori sites.
>
> Twenty minutes later Paul slowed the ute and pulled into a gateway that led to a group of huts. 'This is the camp.'
>
> The light had almost disappeared from the day and pockets of yellow glowed from the huts. The main office sat in darkness so Jeremy hoped they would be able to locate Megan's
> 25   boyfriend quickly because he was tired and hungry.
>
> Extract from *Runaway* by Tania Roxborogh

1   **What was Megan and Jeremy's destination?**

_____

(1 mark)

2   **In the sentence 'All the little townships sprinkled throughout the area sat comfortably at the foot of the Southern Alps' (lines 3 and 4), there are two examples of figurative language. Copy down the image and in your own words explain what it means.**

Image One: _____

Explanation: _____

_____

Image Two: _____

Explanation: _____

(4 marks)

3 In your own words, explain why Jeremy 'felt sure he would have room to grow'.

_____

_____

_____

(1 mark)

4 What is Frog Rock?

_____

_____

(1 mark)

5 What does 'crest' (line 19) mean?

_____

_____

(1 mark)

6 Write down an example of a simile from the passage.

_____

_____

(1 mark)

7 Describe the atmosphere of the final paragraph.

_____

_____

_____

(1 mark)

ISBN: 9780170462990

Passage two

Read the following poem carefully and answer the questions that follow.

Dyed Hair

1   A senior girl in detention last week;
      Her crime?
      Dyed hair.
      I should have been there too,
5   For I am a worse case.
      She dyed her hair for no good reason
      Other than vanity or fashion.
      Me?
      I'm lying – about my age,
10   Cheating – on time,
      Bearing false witness – to my years
      Stealing – back some hope
      How's that for a list?
      So, guard-like, I gave her some books to cover
15   And made sure she completed her sentence;
      No bail allowed.
      Instead, I should have sent her away
      To laugh and sing and dance
      In the freshness of her youth,
20   And sat and covered them myself.

Dorothy Knudson

1 **Why was the senior girl in detention?**

_____

_____

(1 mark)

2 **Who covered the books?**

_____

(1 mark)

3 **'Guard-like' (line 14) is an example of what language feature?**

_____

_____

(1 mark)

4 In your own words, **why did the girl dye her hair?**

_____

_____

_____

(1 mark)

5 **Identify the** metaphor **used in lines 15-16.**

_____

_____

_____

(1 mark)

6 **Explain,** with evidence, **the meaning of the metaphor from question 5.**

_____

_____

_____

_____

_____

_____

(1 mark)

7 **Why does the poet think that she is a 'worse case' than the girl?** Give evidence **from the poem to support your answer.**

_____

_____

_____

_____

_____

_____

(2 marks)

8 **Describe the attitude the poet has toward the senior girl.** Give evidence **from the poem to support your answer.**

_____

_____

_____

_____

(2 marks)

ISBN: 9780170462990   PHOTOCOPYING OF THIS PAGE IS RESTRICTED UNDER LAW.

Passage three

Read the following extract carefully and answer the questions that follow.

What would you do if you found a real mermaid? Would you call the police? The T.V. station? Would you suggest poking it in the eye with a stick? (That was Robbie's idea – not mine).

Well, this is what we did. We took her home. And, we knew pretty quickly it was a 'she' not a 'he' or an 'it' because, unlike those Disney cartoons, mermaids don't have scales and they
5   don't wear cute little shell bras. Mermaids let it all hang out.

We were beachcombing, me and Robbie, because Grandad had said that his beach was excellent for finding things washed up from the liners and cruise ships which pass by. That the current was just right to bring in interesting stuff.

We'd started down the south end of the beach near the twisted Pohutukawa because Grand-
10   dad said that was the best place – it was kind of like a settling pool for the currents. Robbie found a pair of child's glasses; I found a munted Frisbee.

We kept along the high tide mark but swept down toward the water every now and then. About two thirds of the way along the beach, we found her.

"What's that?" Robbie asked, pointing to a fleshy lump huddled amongst the rocks. "Looks
15   like a body."

My stomach squeezed. I wasn't in the mood to find a dead, rotting body on the beach. "We should go get Grandad," I told him. "Probably best to have an adult around."

"Don't be a sissy," Robbie said, giving me one of his looks. My little brother can be really tough sometimes and I knew that this was his way of reminding me, though I was the first born
20   son, he was stronger and tougher than me – even if he was two years and three inches shorter.

I put the Frisbee into the rubbish bag I'd brought along (Grandad's idea) and tucked it under a log so it wouldn't blow away. I was stalling, I knew, but I really didn't want to 'see' what the thing was.

"Charlie," Robbie called, already standing over it. "Check this out. Man!"
25   With my stomach twisting and churning, I strode up to the crop of rocks and the pale, fleshy thing which lay among it.

She was very pale, not white but with a bluey hue. Her eyes were fused shut and sand and salt had dried on her lashes. Her thin lips were almost the same colour as her face – blue-tinged white. Her hair was pulled back into a thick plait and was tangled with seaweed and sand.
30   "You reckon she's dead?" Robbie stared at me, his eyes wide. "Should I poke her?"

I saw him pick up a stick. "No," I hissed at him. "I'll check her pulse." Though I knew already what I would find. There wouldn't be any. It was obvious she was long gone.

Extract from *Charlie Tangaroa and the Creature from the Sea* by T.K. Roxborogh

1

From the information in the passage, explain what beachcombing is?

_____

_____

(1 mark)

_____

2 Describe the relationship between Robbie and Charlie. Give evidence from the passage to support you answer.

_____

_____

(2 marks)

3 In your own words, explain why Charlie suggests that it would be best to get Grandad?

_____

_____

(1 mark)

4 'Let it all hang out.' (line 5) is an example of what style of language?

(1 mark)

_____

_____

5 ' ... sand and salt had dried on her lashes.' (lines 27 and 28) is an example of which language technique?

_____

_____

(1 mark)

6 Write an example of onomatopoeia from the passage.

_____

_____

(1 mark)

7 Create another appropriate title for this extract and explain why you think it is a good title.

_____

_____

(1 mark)

8 Describe the different ways the boys respond to the mermaid.

Charlie: _____

_____

_____

Robbie: _____

_____

_____

(2 marks)

ISBN: 9780170462990

Passage four

Read the following poem carefully and answer the questions that follow.

They Have Cut Down the Pines

They have cut down the pines where they stood;
The wind will miss them – the rain,
When its silver blind is down.
5 They have stripped the bark from the wood –
The needly boughs, and the brown
Knobbly nuts trodden into the ground.
The kind, the friendly trees,
Where all day small winds sound,
10 And all day long the sun
Plays hide and seek with shadows
Till the multiplying shadows turn to one
And night is here.

They have cut down the trees and ended now
15 The gentle colloquy of bough and bough.
They are making the fence by the creek,
And have cut down the pines for the posts.
Wan in the sunlight as ghosts
The naked trunks lie.
20 A bird nested there – it will seek
In vain: they have cut down the pines.

Mary Lisle

colloquy – means conversation
wan – means pale

1   **Why have they cut down the trees?**

_____

_____

_____

_____
                                                 (1 mark)

2   **Why do you think the poet repeats the words 'they have cut down the pines'?**

_____

_____

_____

_____
                                                 (1 mark)

3 What picture of the rain do the words 'its silver blind is down' give you?

(1 mark)

4 'The kind, the friendly trees' ... what poetic device has been used here?

(1 mark)

5 Why are the trunks described as naked?

(1 mark)

6 Give one example of alliteration.

(1 mark)

7 How has the cutting down of the trees affected nature?

(2 marks)

8 Explain how the poet feels about what has just taken place.

(2 marks)

ISBN: 9780170462990